Beautiful
Battlefields

D0029227

Beautiful Battlefields

BO STERN

NAVPRESS
Discipleship Inside Out®

NAVPRESS ⬤

Discipleship Inside Out®

NavPress is the publishing ministry of The Navigators, an international Christian organization and leader in personal spiritual development. NavPress is committed to helping people grow spiritually and enjoy lives of meaning and hope through personal and group resources that are biblically rooted, culturally relevant, and highly practical.

For a free catalog go to www.NavPress.com
or call 1.800.366.7788 in the United States or 1.800.839.4769 in Canada.

© 2013 by Bonita Stern

All rights reserved. No part of this publication may be reproduced in any form without written permission from NavPress, P.O. Box 35001, Colorado Springs, CO 80935. www.navpress.com

NAVPRESS and the NAVPRESS logo are registered trademarks of NavPress. Absence of ® in connection with marks of NavPress or other parties does not indicate an absence of registration of those marks.

ISBN: 978-1-61291-319-3

Cover design by Arvid Wallen
Cover image by Jose AS Reyes

Some of the anecdotal illustrations in this book are true to life and are included with the permission of the persons involved. All other illustrations are composites of real situations, and any resemblance to people living or dead is coincidental.

Unless otherwise identified, all Scripture quotations in this publication are taken from The Holy Bible, English Standard Version (ESV), copyright © 2001 by Crossway Bibles, a division of Good News Publishers. Used by permission. All rights reserved. Other versions used include: the *Amplified Bible* (AMP), © The Lockman Foundation 1954, 1958, 1962, 1964, 1965, 1987; the *Holy Bible, New International Version*® (NIV®), Copyright © 1973, 1978, 1984 by Biblica, used by permission of Zondervan, all rights reserved; the New American Standard Bible® (NASB), Copyright © 1960, 1962, 1963, 1968, 1971, 1972, 1973, 1975, 1977, 1995 by The Lockman Foundation. Used by permission; the Holman Christian Standard Bible (HCSB) ® Copyright © 2003, 2002, 2000, 1999 by Holman Bible Publishers. All rights reserved; the New King James Version (NKJV). Copyright © 1982 by Thomas Nelson, Inc. Used by permission. All rights reserved; *THE MESSAGE* (MSG). Copyright © 1993, 1994, 1995, 1996, 2000, 2001, 2002. Used by permission of NavPress Publishing Group; and the *Holy Bible*, New Living Translation (NLT), copyright © 1996, 2004, 2007. Used by permission of Tyndale House Publishers, Inc., Wheaton, Illinois 60189. All rights reserved.

Stern, Bo.
  Beautiful battlefields / Bo Stern.
    p. cm.
  Includes bibliographical references.
  ISBN 978-1-61291-319-3
  1. Christian life. I. Title.
  BV4909.S74 2013
  248.4--dc23
                                    2012031015

Printed in the United States of America

1 2 3 4 5 6 7 8 / 18 17 16 15 14 13

For Steve.
Friend of God. Love of my life. Bravest man I know.

Contents

PART 2:
STRATEGIES FOR GROWING STRONGER
THROUGH EVERY BATTLE

Acknowledgments

I owe many thanks, much love, and some sort of home-cooked meal to:

Steve Stern: The first to encourage me when I want to give up, to forgive me when I fall, and to lead the parade when I win. Eternity will tell the whole story of the impact your faith has made. Consider this book a head start.

Team Stern: Whitney, Corey, and Greyson Parnell and Victoria, Tess, and Josiah Stern. The six of you have taught me a million lessons in teamwork, trust, loyalty, goodness, and strength this year. You are brave, beautiful examples of God's great work in our world and His incomparable gifts in my life. I adore you.

My mom and dad, Stan and Ellen Mishler: For standing strong in hospital waiting rooms, for constantly believing in the power of Jesus to win this fight, for standing with us in our determination to find beauty in suffering . . . there are not enough thank-yous.

My amazing in-laws, Paul and Eleanor Stern, and the whole Stern/David clan: For staking your flag in the ground of Steve's healing and refusing to budge, for guarding that ground like it was your own patch of lentils, and for raising the most amazing man I know, I am forever in your debt.

Lila Pearson and Cheryl Inman: Dearest sisters, closest friends, fiercest fighters on my battlefield.

Casey Parnell: You are one in a million. Thank you for standing with us through thick and thin.

The army of friends that has enabled me to survive, to stand, and to storm the gates when necessary: Pam Beane, Chris Earwicker, Vangi Taron, Sonja Decker, Nita Belles, Jill Wolfe, Gina Blok, Suzanne Mickel, Kimberly Alexander, Nanci Miller, Deb Gentry, Kristi Dueber, Cathy Parnell, and Tami Sawyer, just to name a few.

My amazing Sometimes Small Group: Mekenzie Stearns, Elisa Earwicker, Stephenie Madsen, Whitney Parnell, Katie Scott, Noel Pearson, and Jenna Javens: You are young, but very wise . . . I love you.

Our pastors, Ken and Linda Johnson: Thank you for always helping us find our way back to a Genesis 50:20 life.

Our trusted team of spiritual leaders and advisors: Steve and Suzanne Mickel, Mike and Kim Alexander, Jim and Jean Stephens, Greg and Karen Fry, John and Sonja Decker.

My agent, Jason Myhre: This is all your fault. Thank you.

Team Steve: Joe Pearson, Dave Inman, Riley Cranston, Scott Robson, Rob Imhoff, Lane Lerhke, Mike Spedick, Beau Crotwell, Kevin Sawyer, Jim Stone, Joe Earwicker, Bob Brown, Louie Hoffman, Dave Blok, Jay Smith, Bob Bolton, Ron Botts (and surely I've forgotten someone). The ways you have loved and cared for Steve could fill a book and probably should. You are men of extraordinary strength and valor. Thank you.

My editor, Liz Heaney: Your skills astound me and your grace blesses me. Thank you for walking me through this process with such finesse. I am so grateful.

To You, Jesus, our prayer remains: *Be glorified. In all our words and ways. In all our hopes and dreams. Be the singular, shining focus of our lives. Because only You are worthy.*

Part 1

DISCOVERING BEAUTY IN THE HARD PLACES

CHAPTER 1

Meeting Goliath

Finding Beauty in the Fight of Your Life

The first shot was fired in the fall.

I love September because it's my birthday month and the start of school. It's a time of year that seems fresh and new and filled with possibility. This particular September day rolled in with the fully alive colors of the season as our mountains welcomed their first sweaters of snow and the orange leaves snapped to attention on the trees. The day could have been perfectly lovely. Except that it turned out to be the day war was declared.

I'm not unfamiliar with the feel of the battlefield. In the course of the average life, plenty of hard times will fall, so on this day, just after having celebrated my forty-fifth birthday, I had already run into my share of bad guys and big losses. I was adept at telling other people how to do battle, and I had confidence in my ability to faith my way through any fight. However, I was about to meet an enemy so fierce and foul that all my previous victories and clever strategies would seem insignificant and impotent by comparison.

Like just about any conflict, this one began long before we realized it. My husband, a man who personifies the word *strapping*, had been experiencing some neck and shoulder weakness that was diagnosed as arthritis and treated with a steroid injection. Weeks later, however, his condition was so much worse that he struggled to hold his head up when he mowed the lawn or rode a bike. Ironically, I was not concerned when I went with him to see a neurologist on that big September day. I have feared pretty much everything else in my life, but our family has been blessed with generations of stout health, and Steve had never had any serious physical issues. To me, he is the strongest man in every room and the definition of stability, so the possibility of a grim diagnosis wasn't even on my radar.

At the clinic, the doctor conducted test after test on Steve's strength, and slowly, steadily, like water seeps into sand, a sense of ominous dread began to roll into that cold, sterile room. Steve had been working hard throughout the year to lose weight and many people had remarked about how great he looked. However, as the neurologist soberly pointed out the lack of symmetry in my husband's twitching shoulder muscles, I realized that what we had assumed was healthy weight loss was actually muscle atrophy.

I can't pinpoint the moment it happened, but at some point during the doctor's silent scrutiny, Goliath walked into the room. Though invisible, his presence was palpable; his size and strength nearly took my breath away. I tried desperately to hold back the tears that were threatening to spill over. Even though the doctor had yet to mention any possible names for whatever was causing Steve to waste away, I knew right then and there that we were in for the fight of our lives. I just knew.

What I wanted to do more than anything was to cry or scream or run like crazy from that doctor's office and pretend this visit had never happened. What I did instead turned out to be a really good decision. I breathed a silent prayer for strength, and the first of at least one million prayers I have prayed for Steve's healing. Then with shaking hands, I sent a text to my sister: *At the dr with Steve and trying not to cry. He's not okay. Please pray.*

As the doctor began explaining the litany of tests that would follow, I could hear his words, but with ears of the spirit I also could hear the sounds of a battle forming. The lines had been drawn. The war was on and the fear felt suffocating. At precisely that moment, I got the text back from Cheryl, *Praying right now!* It didn't answer any questions or change the nature of the fight we were facing. It didn't deal a death blow to Goliath. It did, however, help me to breathe again.

That big day launched a lot of other big days. The day of the EMG (electromyography) to test Steve's nerve/muscle function and discover that, yes, his muscles had atrophied. The day of the first of many MRIs. The day I researched motor neuron diseases and realized that there was no good direction for this situation to go. The dark day that we drove three hours to meet a woman we had never imagined meeting: the director of the ALS center for Providence Hospital. And finally, eight months after the first doctor visit, the day the dreaded diagnosis came: Amyotrophic Lateral Sclerosis. Lou Gehrig's disease.

Each and every one of these moments was an emotional and psychological minefield for our family. I could tell you of hours spent weeping on the floor, telling God that there was no way I could do it . . . no possible way to watch the man I have loved since I was a teenager face the kind of future this diagnosis demands. Or I could tell you about the decision we had to make about whether to spend vast sums of money on a medication that could possibly buy Steve an extra three months of life. Or even about the small tasks that needed to be handled, like finding the right way to "bank" Steve's voice so that it can be used instead of a computer voice when he needs to move to an augmentative speech device. Nearly every decision we have faced has packed an emotional wallop the likes of which we have never had to absorb before. I've gotten plenty of sympathy and hugs, so please know that I am not saying this to gain more, but rather to help you feel and smell the ground on which our family fights: This has been, without any close second, the most intense and excruciating battle we have ever faced.

However, and this is a *big* however, God Himself has come to our crisis. He has shown up in miraculous and magnificent ways, and this has caused an indelible change in one specific area of my thinking. I used to believe that God could bring good things from hard times, almost like a cosmic consolation prize for having endured something unfortunate or unfair. Now that I've walked with Him this far through this fight, I am certain of this one truth: Some beautiful things can *only* be found in the hardest times. Can you turn that idea around in your mind for a bit and let its size and scope seep in? God is *for* us. He is for our growth, our joy, our success, and our maturity, and He will use every struggle we face as the delivery agents for His most remarkable gifts. Our beautiful God has hidden beauty in the soil of our battlefield. He has placed treasure there that we simply would not be able to find in other, more peaceful places.

Before we faced this fight, I knew this truth in theory, but I hadn't experienced a fire hot enough to prove and refine it. Now I can say with great confidence, I *own* it. On good days and on bad, in war and in peace, in sickness and in health, I know in the deepest part of my heart that He is the God who brings beauty from battle.

I have seen this principle play out firsthand as I've experienced countless miracle moments of unexpected joy and supernatural strength while on the battlefield. Mornings when I didn't think I could get out of bed, God has appeared in the form of a phone call or e-mail from a friend who stepped in to extend His hand so I could stand. Sometimes the help came in the form of a box on my desk, wrapped in Disney princess paper. Inside? A whole box of Twinkies. I really, really love Twinkies even though I know I shouldn't. Another day it was yellow tulips. On my anniversary it was an office filled to overflowing with gifts and flowers from the women who love me and knew it would be a rough day. These small-yet-supernatural notes from God have shown up strategically to remind me that He knows me enough to send someone to speak my language.

And also, He comes Himself. In the dark of night when it's just me and my tears and fears and *what ifs* and *why mes*, He shows up. Through His voice, His Word, and His indescribable but absolutely undeniable presence, He has strengthened me and proven Himself sure and steadfast. Every. Single. Time. I can say with confidence: This battle is not destroying us. In fact, in the midst of this trauma and turmoil, God's power to use every bad thing for our good is making us more beautiful than we have ever been.

This is the landscape of my fight, and I'm guessing that you have a fight too.

WHAT ABOUT YOU?

I am convinced that everyone, at some point on the journey between here and eternity, will face a Really Big Battle. Most of us can easily reach into our memory bank and remember the moment the battle lines were drawn.

My friend Vickie can still hear the loud ring of the first shot while she was in the hospital delivery room and the doctor whisked her baby off to intensive care before she could even get a good look. Hours later, she would learn that they were facing the giant of Down syndrome.

Jill recalls the moment like it was yesterday. A note from the city on the door of their twenty-year-old family business informed them that, because of a legal technicality, the building no longer belonged to them. When the dust settled, her family was left without a business, a home, and nearly all of the material security they had once known.

Debbie suspected a battle was looming because her husband kept going to the doctor but wouldn't tell her why. The shot rang out on the day she happened to be driving a few cars behind him and watched in horror as his van began to swerve in and out of his lane. When he finally pulled over, she ran to his side and found that he was having a seizure. She would later learn it was the result of cancer that had metastasized to his brain.

Do you remember a day when you heard a shot ring out and you realized you were in a battle for your joy, your marriage, your finances, your health . . . your future? Maybe you are engaged in something fairly fierce right this minute and are looking for hope that you will breathe again, laugh again, trust God again. Perhaps you are wondering why you are still standing. Or maybe you are on the other side of your battle, but it cost you nearly everything, and you're trying valiantly to believe that God is for you and with you, even though you feel quite desperately alone. I understand, friend. Oh, how I do.

THIS IS ABOUT TO GET BEAUTIFUL

My Goliath is an insidious motor neuron disease and all the emotional, physical, and financial implications that go along with it, but so many different battles rage around us every day. I have run into plenty of women who are also fighting a Really Big Battle, and you will meet some of them in this book. I've also been studying the battle stories in the Bible, looking for principles that can help me in this fight. Nearly all the heroes of our faith were tested, trained, and made stronger through their time on the fighting fields. These glorious, victorious examples from the past and the present are teaching me that war is hell, but God is good. And He who is the great Giver of every good gift creates some of the most brilliant and beautiful things in the darkest, most daunting seasons. He does. I promise.

If our roles were reversed, and you were telling me your story, I know that together we could find something beautiful that you have already gathered in the course of your fight. I'm also willing to bet that with a few intentional but relatively simple adjustments, you could find yourself with more treasure than your arms could hold or your heart contain, not in spite of your battle, but *because* of it. But finding that treasure is a trick sometimes. It can be difficult because so often we invest so much energy in surviving a battle that there's little left for discovering what wonderful things might have happened inside of us in the process. My deepest hope is that this book will help you do just that.

As we travel together through part 1, we'll look for treasure. We'll sift through the soil of the battleground to discover the gold that glistens beneath the surface. Once we know it's there, the next step is to face our fight with faith and ask, *How do I win this thing?* Part 2 will focus on battle-proven strategies for winning the battle. Now, for our purposes, "winning" doesn't necessarily mean that God has worked everything out as we had hoped (though it sometimes happens that way). It means that God has worked everything *together* to make us stronger, better, and more beautiful. Do you have faith to believe that you could walk off this battlefield more alive and free and ready to face your future than you have ever been before? Please, believe it. It's possible, friend.

I don't know exactly what you're facing today, but I want you to know that I am praying for you. I know that you've scraped together all your courage just to open the cover of a book that promises this fantastic opportunity to revisit the battle-ravaged country of your soul. I am praying for you. That life will spring from the pages, His voice will ring in your ears, and you will know for certain that the Captain and Commander is bringing life from ashes, order from chaos, strength from pain. I am praying for you. That the tears you cry as you walk this road will bring healing as they flow and will usher in hope for a new and lovely season where laughter is not a rare guest, but a welcomed friend. I am praying for you. And I want you to know it.

Let's find some beauty, shall we?

WORTH PONDERING

1. Think about the current battle(s) you face. If you had to give your fight an epic name, what would it be?
2. If we were talking over coffee right now, I would ask you this question: "If you had to tell me one thing you have discovered or one way you have grown through this battle that wouldn't have been possible another way, what would it be?" Now answer that question.

WORTH DOING

Write the word *beautiful* on a sticky note and place it on your mirror, your Bible, your computer monitor—anyplace you will regularly see it. This little prompt will remind you that He loves you and is building something beautiful in you through your battle.

CHAPTER 2

The G50:20 Principle

The Beauty of Life-Changing Purpose

Tears rolled down her face and onto my shirt sleeves. She had been waiting a long time after a conference to speak with me, and by the time she made it to the front of the line, all she could do was hug me and cry. My heart broke as she wept. When at last she could speak, her story came out in a tumble of words and still more tears.

She had been sexually abused for the first ten years of her life, which represented half of all the years she had lived so far. As soon as she was able, she had moved out of her home and in with a boy who had given her a baby and a lot of heartache before walking out on her. Two years later, she had a good job, a daughter she adored, and a group of friends and family who cared deeply for her. A combination of hard work and some good breaks had helped her turn her life around into a remarkable success story, yet she could not stop weeping. And she kept saying over and over again, "Ten years. Ten years were stolen from me and I can never get them back. Why would this happen? Why would God ever let this happen?"

Surely one of the most difficult and weighty aspects of facing a big fight in life is dealing with the question *Why me?* I'm certain that for every person, the question is framed a little differently, but for most of us, it begs to be asked.

Sometimes the answers seem obvious. A friend's husband fought lung disease that eventually took his life, leaving her with a broken heart and young children to raise. I spoke with her about it during his battle, and she shook her head sadly and said, "Well, he smoked for years." For her, the *Why him?* question had a clear answer, and while she was still devastated over the situation, she had some comfort in being able to pin down a reason. I don't, however, think it's that straightforward for many of us.

ALS is a disease that has no known cause and seems to be random in its selection process. Sometimes when I see stories on the news of people who do wicked things to their families or to our world, I look at the good life my husband has tried to live and I wonder, *Why Steve?* I'm not proud of that question and I don't think anyone deserves a disease, but I would be lying if I said I hadn't hurled some questions up to the heavens about the fairness of it all.

One of the primary questions posed by those who doubt the existence of God is, why would He let bad things happen to good people? For the first forty-five years of my life, I was able to spout off glib answers to this question, but on the day that I felt the first pangs of real suffering, it wasn't as simple anymore. This fight forced me to get very real and very aggressive with the question of *Why?* Sometimes I think we hide our doubts or pretend they don't exist, or we use them as an excuse to walk away from a God whose ways seem too mysterious to understand. But I don't think God is afraid of our questions. He will respond to the heart that cries out to Him for answers. Our fight with ALS has led me to knock on His door and keep knocking. It has led me to ask and keep asking. It has pushed me to identify the things that I really, truly believe about the purpose of suffering so that I can build on truth in the middle of this battle.

CONNECTING THE DOTS

Why do bad things happen to good people? I found the answer I was looking for in the life of a man in a prison uniform. Genesis is an interesting book because the first part covers a lot of ground. The plot moves quickly through several generations until chapter 37, when we can almost hear the screeching of the author's pen as he slows to a crawl to look at the life of Joseph's family in vivid detail. The remaining fourteen chapters of Genesis are devoted to Joseph's story.

He was the son of the patriarch Jacob and his favorite wife, Rachel. When you're the eleventh of twelve sons, you learn all sorts of tricks for getting attention, and Joseph was no different. He tattled on his brothers to his father and then received a beautifully woven coat, which seemed to underscore his status as Daddy's favorite. His older brothers were already miffed by their dad's favoritism, but then Joseph made it worse by telling them about a dream in which they bowed down to him. Really bad idea. Either Joseph was seriously lacking in social intuition, or he was deliberately arrogant in his behavior with his brothers. He even managed to infuriate his father with his talk of dreams and sheaves and stars.

Finally, the brothers had enough and they sold Joseph to slave traders, telling their father that he was killed by an animal. I've heard this story since I was a little girl and have read it more times than I can count, but for some reason this section of it has become very real to me recently. I can imagine young Joseph like I can see my own son, Josiah. I can see him being stripped of the coat that he loved, thrown in an empty well, and probably thinking he would die there. I can hear the sounds of the twenty shekels being tossed to his brothers by the Midianites, and I can see Joseph being pulled behind their caravan — the favorite son, now a slave. We already know the end of the story, so it's easy to gloss over the pain and heartache woven throughout, but make no mistake: Joseph endured the deepest kind of rejection and betrayal.

He was carried away to Egypt, where he was sold to a man named Potiphar. This is where the story gets really interesting because it seems that, even though Joseph was betrayed by his brothers and was dead to his dad, he was seen and known and loved by God (and so are you). God was with him so strongly that everything in Potiphar's house prospered because of Joseph. However, Joseph once again fell from grace when Potiphar believed his wife's false accusations that Joseph had tried to rape her.

In one fell swoop, and through no fault of his own, Joseph went from man-in-charge to man-in-chains. Living in prison, he was probably surrounded by people who were in jail for good reason, while he was there for doing the right thing. Surely he was tempted to wonder, *Why me?* I think I would have felt desperately alone and unloved. I would have shaken my fists at the heavens, wondering where God had gone. But, as Joseph soon discovered, God had not gone anywhere. Look at this:

> The LORD was with Joseph and showed him steadfast love and gave him favor in the sight of the keeper of the prison. And the keeper of the prison put Joseph in charge of all the prisoners who were in the prison. Whatever was done there, he was the one who did it. The keeper of the prison paid no attention to anything

that was in Joseph's charge, because the LORD was with him. And whatever he did, the LORD made it succeed. (Genesis 39:21-23)

Here's what I love about this section of the story, and it applies to all of us in any battle: Even though circumstances seem to be against him, the Lord was with Joseph. He was in prison, but he was not out of favor. This fact is a flashing arrow or a neon sign telling us that *something bigger is going on here.*

Joseph was eventually promoted right out of that cell and into Pharaoh's court when he was asked to interpret a dream Pharaoh had that no one else could figure out. Because God was with Joseph, he had no trouble understanding that the dream foretold that the world would undergo seven years of plenty, followed by seven years of famine. Pharaoh rewarded Joseph by making him second-in-command in all of Egypt so that he could prepare the land for the coming famine. Under Joseph's direction, the Egyptians stored up provision for seven years.

Then one day during the famine, Joseph's brothers appeared before him, hoping to get some of that stored provision in order to feed their families back in Canaan. They were now beggars on the doorstep of the brother they had sold into slavery so many years earlier. Joseph's dream had at last come true, but I'm guessing it looked a lot different than he thought it would look from the other side of his suffering. Even though it is easy for us to trace our finger along the trail of God's sovereignty in Joseph's life, that was not the case for Joseph in the midst of his battles. It wasn't until the end of the story that he caught a glimpse of what God was doing. The following verses make it clear that the beautiful rewards from this battle came at the cost of many tears:

- "His father wept for him" (Genesis 37:35, HCSB).
- "He was overcome with emotion for his brother, and he was about to weep" (43:30, HCSB).

- "He wept so loudly that the Egyptians heard it, and also Pharaoh's household heard it" (45:2, HCSB).
- "Then Joseph threw his arms around Benjamin and wept, and Benjamin wept on his shoulder" (45:14, HCSB).
- "Joseph kissed each of his brothers as he wept" (45:15, HCSB).
- "Joseph presented himself to him, threw his arms around him, and wept for a long time" (46:29, HCSB).
- "Then Joseph, leaning over his father's face, wept and kissed him" (50:1, HCSB).

Despite the number of years, tears, and sleepless nights this fight had taken from him, Joseph was able to answer the big, brooding question, *Why me?* He managed—in just one sentence—to connect the dots from his deep pain to God's great purpose: "But Joseph said to them, 'Don't be afraid. Am I in the place of God? You intended to harm me, but God intended it for good to accomplish what is now being done, the saving of many lives'" (Genesis 50:19-20, NIV).

Notice that Joseph did not tell his brothers, "God intended this for good so that I could be a big shot in the government" or "God intended this for good so that I would be vindicated and you would be embarrassed." No. Joseph understood that everything leading to this moment had been intended for one purpose only: the saving of many lives. If not for the providence of God, which used an unlikely string of events to place the right man in power at the right time, countless people would have died of starvation. It really is true: Something bigger was going on behind the scenes of Joseph's battle.

I call this the Genesis 50:20 principle, and it has been part of the beauty Steve and I have found in this fight. It is powerfully effective in blasting through self-pity and any questions we might have about God's love or care for us. We know that Satan intended this sickness for evil. But we also know in the depths of our souls that God is using it to accomplish something bigger than our eyes can see . . . even something bigger than our minds can conceive.

SAYING YES TO HIS PURPOSES

An amazing army of believers has surrounded us throughout this fight, which is an invaluable gift to us. However, with them also comes an army of ideas about the way our "win" should look. The strongest opinions have been offered by those who feel the only acceptable outcome in this battle is miraculous healing. Folks who hold this view fervently believe that anything other than that would be less than God's best. Some have felt that our focus on learning and growing through suffering is a weak substitute for what God really wants to do, which is to show His power through supernatural physical intervention. "What a testimony that would be to unbelievers," they say, and I agree. Healing is a powerful sign to the world that God is real and strong and compassionate, and I am praying for healing every day. However, I don't believe it's the *only* way that God shows His goodness or demonstrates His love for us. As difficult as it is for me to admit, God's purpose is not necessarily to work everything out for Steve and Bo. His purpose remains for us today as it was for Joseph: the saving of many lives.

Does that sound unfair? Does it seem a little mean for God to use Steve's suffering to bring hope to those who have none? I don't think it is. On the day we realized that we were in for the fight of our lives, Steve and I sat together on our sofa, tears streaming, and said, "We are lashed to the altar of God's purpose, no matter what." We said yes to this, to whatever He allows, to wherever His purpose takes us.

So, where has God's purpose taken us? Oh, so many

beautiful places. Steve's diagnosis opened our hearts to a community of people we didn't really know anything about, and He has given us enormous love for them. We felt pity for those with ALS before, but now we *love* them. In fact, as I write these words, I am fighting to see through the tears and breathe through the ache in my chest as I think of the brave men and women who have become so dear to us. For most of our lives, we have loved and served people in the church, but this battle has moved us into new places, and the community of faith has come right along with us. We watched in awe one bright Saturday morning as a team of four hundred people, mostly from our church, showed up to walk in support of ALS families in our region. They raised money and flipped pancakes and wore Team Stern T-shirts as their feet moved outside the church and into a world where hurting people need to know that they are seen and known and loved by God. Of the hundreds who walked on our team, only a handful had ever been involved in raising awareness for ALS before. This walk has been happening for many years in our community, but it was invisible to us until we found ourselves sharing in this suffering.

Recently we attended a big fund-raising event for ALS research. Hundreds of people in cocktail attire filled a ballroom, ready to write big checks for a great cause that was represented that night by five or six PALS (People with ALS). The PALS congregated together in the lobby, and all but Steve were in wheelchairs. Most could no longer speak, but it didn't matter because our hearts spoke the same language. We shared something deep — an invisible thread that joined us together in understanding. I have studied theology for twenty-five years and have been on staff at a church for ten, but I have never felt more purpose-driven than I do when we are working to serve the ALS community. Steve and I don't feel like victims; we feel commissioned by God to love, support, and pray for those whose suffering we understand because we share it.

Every week, Steve gets phone calls from men who are searching for hope. They are emotionally or spiritually sick and looking for resurrection life. Their marriages are dying or their kids are struggling or they are strangled by addictions and don't know how to find freedom. These men call my husband and pour out their hearts over coffee, and when Steve speaks, they listen. He tells them the truth because he knows that unless God heals him, time could be short, and they listen because they know it too. Steve met with men with the very same problems before his diagnosis, but it's different now. He says that people are inclined to believe him because, "A man with a death sentence has nothing to lose." Lives are being changed and saved because of the battle we are facing.

It's not an easy road to walk, but we keep returning to the truth we have always known and owned: God will not be in debt to us. He is working everything together for His great glory and our great good. It's His way. He isn't sacrificing Steve's life for the lives of others; He is *using* Steve's life in ways that we have never dreamed possible and producing fruit that might have otherwise been inaccessible. God is, in short, answering the cry of our hearts by using us to extend His love to our world and by walking us *through* affliction, rather than around it.

Did God give Steve ALS? No. God hates ALS. Can He work this temporary affliction into an eternal weight of glory? Absolutely. He can. He is. I promise.

How might God be working in and through your battle to bring about the saving of many lives? Maybe it's impossible to imagine that anyone could be reached or won to Love by your struggle, but you will be amazed by what can happen when you say yes. When we are willing to let God use our deepest pain to show His goodness to those who are watching, remarkable things can happen.

FOLLOWING OUR GRIEF TO JESUS

I've heard people say that their goal is to become famous so they have a huge platform on which to share the gospel. I've heard others say that they are hoping to become very wealthy so they can support many ministries and missionaries who will win many to Jesus. On a smaller scale, we often imagine people looking at our happy lives and saying, "What is it that's so different about your life than mine?" thereby creating a perfect opening to share God's story with those poor folks whose lives aren't working.

We too often forget that people will also follow our *grief* to get to Jesus. They will watch us on the day our spouse walks out the door or the business goes bankrupt or the child runs away or we receive an ominous diagnosis. They will watch . . . and they will look to see if the God we preached on our best day can sustain us on the hardest one. Many people cannot relate to outrageous success, but they can relate to tears and brokenness and sorrow. We all suffer, but those who know Christ should suffer with hope so that a watching world can see that He is a very present help in times of trouble. We may wish for a God who will keep us out of all affliction, but isn't it wonderful to become acquainted with the One who goes with us into the heart of the fight, and then uses it for something beautiful?

Still, as much as I believe and understand this concept, it's not easy for me to remember the answer to the question, *Why Steve? Why me? Why our family?* It was hard to remember on the day our son realized he would have to play basketball with his mom from now on. It was hard on the day that Steve retired from work, fifteen years ahead of schedule. It's hard nearly every time I see an elderly couple walking hand in hand and I suddenly find my eyes blurry with tears. I'm really human, and it's really hard. So I recently had a ring made as a reminder, and I wear it all the time. It is inscribed with my husband's name and Genesis 50:20. In the darkest moments, I look at the ring and remember: God's purpose is to save *many* lives, and He will accomplish that through us as we stay aligned with His will, both on and off the battlefield.

God is outrageously good, and He is not just using us to bless His world; He is also meeting our needs. In the next chapter we'll look at the ways He provides, and we'll build some solid reasons for trusting Him in battle.

WORTH PONDERING

1. Read the story of Joseph in Genesis 37, 39–47 and write down or discuss the things — negative and positive — he experienced.
2. What are some similarities between Joseph's battles and those you have faced (rejection, betrayal, broken family relationships, false accusations, and so on)?

WORTH DOING

Think of several people you know who have been through a Really Big Battle and seem more beautiful because of it. How has their fight influenced your life? Write down all the ways God might be using your battle to save others.

Catching Manna

The Beauty of Miraculous Provision

I recently asked a group of young women who had never been married what they believed was the most important quality in a potential spouse. The most popular answer by a landslide was "a good sense of humor." Next, I asked some of my friends who have been through the battle of divorce the same question. This time, the number one answer was a resounding "trustworthiness." Having experienced the reality that unfolds after the fairy-tale wedding is over, these women know that being able to trust the man they marry is essential for any sort of success. "If I want to laugh, I'll watch a sitcom," one smart woman said, "but I *marry* a man I know I can count on."

Now, I know the younger women are not asserting that a funny man is better than a trustworthy one. Rather, they're assuming that loving a man and trusting him go hand in hand. Experience has taught the older women that this is not always the case.

The older I get, the more I understand that trust and love are not the interlocking attributes I once thought they were. Both are essential but they are not the same, and of the two, love is probably easier to do. If you were to group the people in your life into those you love and those you know you can trust when the chips are down, you'll probably find the first group is much larger than the second one.

Earning trust and trusting others are both difficult to do. Maybe that's because we understand our own humanity so well. We know that while a friend or spouse may want to be reliable, they will sometimes lack the ability or the character to pull it off. And even if they do manage it, sometimes our own painful track record causes us to ration out trust sparingly so as not to get burned.

Trust is hard. It's even hard with God. For years I have said that I love Him, but this season of struggle has revealed how important it is that I can confidently depend on Him. Trust is intimate. It develops in the dark places and difficult moments of our lives and is one of the beautiful treasures we discover when we are on the battlefield.

FROM HIS HAND TO MY THIRSTY HEART

The day after Steve's diagnosis, I sat in my favorite chair in my home office and tried to convince myself the room wasn't spinning. It wasn't the room; it was my *life*.

My hope.

My expectations.

Everything was spinning, and spinning makes me feel sick and scared. In that moment, I was worried about a long list of issues: Steve, money, kids, ministry, friends. Everything. Finally, I abandoned all my self-constructed togetherness and did the crying I had been putting off for twenty-four hours. Grief hit like a hurricane. Facedown on the floor, I heaved out sobs of fear and sorrow so deep that even my faithful border collie left the room. All I knew for sure was that I was desperate to hear God. I needed Him to show up on my battlefield. At one point, I even pressed my ear into the carpet, listening for His footsteps, listening for anything that sounded like hope. And then, like the faint pinging of a ship on the radar, I heard two words. Just two words that kept coming over and over again, first like gentle waves on the shore and then with a stronger force and steady cadence.

Every minute. Every minute. Every minute . . .

I wondered what they meant. Maybe that God would be with me every minute? Nope. While I knew that was true, I also knew that wasn't what those two words meant. I opened my laptop and wrote them out over and over again, and then I stared at them on the screen. *Every minute.* Slowly, the deeper meaning of those words began to fall like glistening raindrops from God's hand to my thirsty heart. When I set my fingers on the keyboard again, the words tumbled out: *I have already been to every minute you will ever face. I have been to your future and back, and I have built provision in every minute where you will need it. You won't see it now, but it will be there when you get there.*

I thought about that for a bit and then realized I wasn't worrying about provision for that particular minute. In that moment I had everything I needed. I was worrying about all the minutes that would come. And then, like the sun peeking up over the mountains in the morning, this assurance began to shine over Steve's dark diagnosis: God goes before me, so I never go anywhere first. He already knows where the days will lead and how the battle will turn out, and He has placed all the supplies we will need along the way. I'll see them when we get there.

THE GOD WHO GOES BEFORE

Trusting God is difficult because most often the provision we need is not packed up in a suitcase that is handed to us when we arrive on the battlefield. Instead, He has given us everything we will ever need in His promise that He has gone before us.

Isaiah tells us, "The past events have indeed happened. Now I declare new events; I announce them to you before they occur" (42:9, HCSB). How does God know about these events before they happen? Because He lives outside our timeline and can see from Genesis to Revelation and back again. Beginning to end, it all belongs to Him. He lives ahead of our battle and knows exactly where it is going.

David caught this idea too when he said, "Your eyes saw me when I was formless; all my days were written in Your book and planned before a single one of them began" (Psalm 139:16, HCSB). The psalmist understood that he was not living in a random, spinning storyline, nor was he the victim of circumstance or fickle fate. He was living the prepenned pages of a beautifully crafted narrative written by a God who already knew the end when He wrote the very first word.

God has also written the Book of Bo and the Book of Steve and the Book of You. The God who knows the whole story can be trusted with all the days that fill its pages, but it's always tempting to pick up the pen ourselves. When it seems like the plotline is spinning out of control or when the hero is taking too long to arrive on the scene, I want to take over. I want to make my own happy ending, or at least take a sneak peek at the postbattle pages so that I know everything will turn out okay if I trust Him with my life.

I'm finding, though, that He is a page-by-page, line-by-line God. He shows up in every word, in every syllable, and He proves Himself trustworthy every time. And in the process of watching the story unfold, I am drawn closer to His presence and more fully dependent on His provision.

THE GIFT OF DAILY BREAD

Our faithful Father has been helping His children trust in His provision since the beginning of time. We see this in His dealings with the Israelites when they were wandering in the wilderness.

The children of Israel marched out of their former lives of slavery in Egypt and into a new and unknown land. They had Moses as their leader, a sign in the sky for direction, and that's pretty much it. En route to the Promised Land, they saw magnificent miracles and experienced big wins on the battlefield, but still they regularly returned to this question: Will God provide?

In Exodus 16, we find the people complaining to Moses because they were worried about what they would eat. The text doesn't tell us that they were actually hungry, only that they were afraid of being hungry: "Would that we had died by the hand of the LORD in the land of Egypt, when we sat by the meat pots and ate bread to the full, for you have brought us out into this wilderness to kill this whole assembly with hunger" (verse 3).

Let's pause for a moment and remember that the Israelites were following the God who had turned out all the lights in Egypt for three days, sent hail like missiles to free His people from Pharaoh, and blown back the waters of the Red Sea.[1] God had proven His ability *and* His intention to protect His people time and time again, yet they still struggled to trust Him for provision.

God responded to their complaint by sending food from the sky and then telling them they could store up food only for the

Sabbath. One day each week they were allowed to take more than they needed, but otherwise they were to live day to day, trusting that He would provide what they needed. Of course, they broke the rule (I would have too), and they quickly discovered that God was in charge not only of sending the manna but also of spoiling it (see Exodus 16:20).

Every time I read this story, it's clear to me that God was realigning the mind-set of the Israelites, moving them away from their dependency on Egypt and their own abilities in order to establish their full confidence in His ability to give them everything they would ever need. As they learned to trust God for daily bread, they were learning to lean on His lordship in brand-new ways. How easy would it have been for the God of the universe to stockpile the Israelites with bread and meat for a year? In His infinite wisdom, He chose instead to feed them day by day, giving them 365 opportunities to trust Him.

Much later in their journey, Moses spoke these words as the Israelites prepared to enter the Promised Land, and I have adopted them as my very own battle cry:

> Do not be in dread or afraid of them. The LORD your God *who goes before you* will himself fight for you, just as he did for you in Egypt before your eyes, and in the wilderness, where you have seen how the LORD your God carried you, as a man carries his son, all the way that you went until you came to this place. (Deuteronomy 1:29-31, emphasis added)

Isn't that lovely? Moses knew that the Israelites didn't get to this point on their own; they were carried by God like a dad carries his child when he grows too weary to walk. Because God had faithfully provided all they needed, the children of Israel could rest in the knowledge that He would not disappoint them now. He had proven His character in the wilderness; He would be faithful in this new fight for the Promised Land.

PERFECT AND PUNCTUAL PROVISION

As we face battles of all kinds, we'll find that the same God who daily sustained the Israelites can be trusted with our lives as well.

For many years Linda fought to stay safe in an abusive marriage, but the day finally came when she knew that God had given her the green light to move her family out of the pain of her husband's alcoholism and anger and into a new life. It wasn't easy. Walking out on the abuse also meant leaving her home, security, reputation, and credit score. Leaving one battle behind meant facing a new battlefield where she would need to trust God for everything.

Linda knew that it was time to develop an unshakable reliance on Jesus, the only One who could heal and rebuild her family. Having no idea how it would all work out, and feeling that her prayers kept turning into panicked pleading, she set her heart to worship. With an iPod full of worship music as her day-and-night companion, she found that she was becoming tethered to a new awareness of God's character and, consequently, a new sense of trust in His ability to provide for her and her children. She worshipped as she lost her home. She worshipped as she gave up the ministry positions she had loved. She worshipped as she walked her children through their pain and sorrow. And as she humbled herself in front of the God who makes all things new, He began to provide in supernaturally beautiful ways.

Provision didn't gush out like water from a bucket, but rather like the steady summer rain that falls on a warm evening, refreshing the earth and refilling wells. As Linda leaned fully on God's promise to provide, He showed up on time, every time. She was blessed with just the right house at just the right moment. Out of the blue, she was asked to step into a ministry opportunity that perfectly utilized her passions and kept her connected to the Word of God in ways she wouldn't have been otherwise. Relationships fell into place that gave her strength, hope, and companionship. Day by day, she found that He was placing pieces where they needed to go and was working those pieces together to create something more beautiful than she ever could have imagined. Now, many years later, her life has come full circle. She radiates a confidence born in the battle. She is a woman who knows that God has gone before her into every minute, and so she's not afraid to follow Him into all that is to come.

I, too, am finding that I can trust God to provide. Part of the nature of a disease like ALS is that it slowly but surely changes every aspect of a person's existence. At the point of diagnosis, most people are still living relatively normal lives, but it quickly becomes a daunting task to get up each morning, wondering what muscle might not be working today. Steve initially went to the doctor because he was having trouble with his golf swing. Six months later, I watched his hand shake as he tried to lift his fork to his mouth at breakfast. It's a difficult decline, so if I let myself, I could spend most of my time worrying about what is yet to come and wondering how we will face the days that look impossible.

Through trial, error, and a lot of practice, I am learning to keep my eyes and heart living in the day at hand and trust God for all that we will face in the future. We are choosing to trust that the pages of our story have been written by the One who loves us deeply and that no other pen can alter His plan. This is the greatest assurance we have that we will win this fight.

Taped to my bathroom mirror is this beautiful quote by Civil War chaplain E. M. Bounds:

When we pray, "Give us this day our daily bread," we are, in a measure, shutting tomorrow out of our prayer. We do not live in tomorrow but in today. We do not seek tomorrow's grace or tomorrow's bread. . . . Bread, for today, is bread enough. Bread given for today is the strongest sort of pledge that there will be bread tomorrow.[2]

All that God has given us today assures us that He will still be on the job tomorrow. His love will not shift or change, and His provision will be steady and true.

Whatever the nature of your battle, I am certain you could build your own shortcut or a long, safe-looking detour if you want to. (I've done it myself more times than I can count.) But I am equally certain that if you choose instead to stay committed to God's purpose and to focus on His presence, you will find that you are not the first to arrive in this harrowing, holy battleground. God always goes ahead and provides for our needs, so we never have to go alone. This is all the hope we need for every minute of the journey. He is, of all things, trustworthy. And He also has a great sense of humor.

Next up: Have you ever experienced a moment on the battle-field when you wished a superhero would show up? Well, I have good news for you, friend.

WORTH PONDERING
1. In what ways has your battle caused you to worry about the future?
2. Think of all the ways, small and big, you have seen evidence that God has gone before you?
3. How does a minute-by-minute dependence upon God's provision affect your relationship with Him?

WORTH DOING

This week, each time you see or hear a clock, stop to breathe a little prayer of thanks that He's already been to the next minute and you won't be going there alone.

CHAPTER 4

In the Shadow of a Superhero

The Beauty of Supernatural Strength

Our three daughters are quite different from each other. Whitney is blonde. Victoria is brunette. Tess has delightfully, definitely red hair. While they're all smart and funny, each has her own style, ranging from quiet to quirky. One loves music, one loves photography, one loves to write. They are each unique, but they have a common boogeyman: spiders.

The younger Stern women detest them. They abhor them. They fervently fight against the right of spiders to live. Problem is, our girls aren't brave enough to face them alone, so when Steve or I get a text late at night, we never assume it's from a needy friend. We know without a doubt that it is from a daughter who needs us to come to her bedroom and kill a spider. Steve will always comply. He will get dressed and go downstairs and fight the bad bug for the daughter he loves.

I have been asking myself why we fear what we fear, and I think it's because we, like my daughters, blow up the size of our opponent, whether it's a bad diagnosis, a big financial challenge, or even Satan himself. When we do this, we feel small and impotent by comparison. And, in truth, some giants are huge and intimidating. What we are forgetting is that we are not in this battle alone. We have Someone who will fight our battle for us.

THE BEAUTY OF A BIG OPPONENT

David understood this. He wrote, "He reached from on high, He took me; He drew me out of many waters. He delivered me from my strong enemy and from those who hated and abhorred me, for they were too strong for me" (Psalm 18:16-17, AMP).

David knew that some guys were bigger and badder than he was. Some of them were too strong for him. But they were not too strong for his Dad. Oh, how I can relate! Long before our current battle began, I wrote this in the margin of my Bible next to this verse: "David knows he couldn't have done this on his own. That's the beauty of a big opponent—we see the strength and size of God."

Fast-forward a couple of years and I'm also facing a giant who is much bigger than any I have ever imagined, and I am discovering I was right. A big enemy reveals the power of God in ways I've never seen before. I have always loved Him, but I never realized how big I would need Him to be until we entered this battle.

One of the hidden treasures we can find on the battlefield is the ability to clearly see the strength of the One who fights for us. In fact, look at what the psalmist says about the way our enemies view our God: "Say to God, 'How awe-inspiring are Your works!

Your enemies will cringe before You because of Your great strength'" (Psalm 66:3, HCSB).

Our enemies cringe before God because of His great strength. I wonder if we understand this, because I think if we did, we would be very brave.

Psalm 18 lists God's enemy-fighting ways, and they are intense.

> The LORD also thundered in the heavens,
>> and the Most High uttered his voice,
>> hailstones and coals of fire.
> And he sent out his arrows and scattered them;
>> he flashed forth lightnings and routed them.
> Then the channels of the sea were seen,
>> and the foundations of the world were laid bare
> at your rebuke, O LORD,
>> at the blast of the breath of your nostrils.
>
> He sent from on high, he took me;
>> he drew me out of many waters.
> He rescued me from my strong enemy
>> and from those who hated me,
>> for they were too mighty for me. (verses 13-17)

Wow. Somebody's enemy is in trouble; I would like for it to be mine! When I read this description of the way that God comes to rescue, I wonder if we have overly domesticated Him. He comes breathing fire, parting clouds, shooting hailstones and thunderbolts, and yet we live in fear of our enemies. We have constructed an image of a meek and lowly Jesus and have turned Him into a house god that sits on our mantle and is in charge of keeping the kids safe and our budget running smoothly. Until we are faced with a larger-than-life opponent, an enemy far outside of our weight class, we will never need to see the true power of the God we have chosen to serve.

We should be done with the days of believing that God's power is evidenced primarily by the absence of struggle in our lives. If we live any amount of time in this fallen and frustrating world, we are going to find ourselves stepping onto the soil of some intense battlefields. We will face some dauntingly large enemies who are bent on our destruction. If we hold them up next to our own strength, we will be scared right out of our shoes. But if we compare them to our powerful God, we will realize that these conflicts are a gift because small enemies equal small victories and huge enemies equal huge wins.

THE "ENOUGHNESS" OF GOD

I have interviewed a variety of amazing women about their battlefields. Apart from having experienced extraordinarily difficult things in life, few other parallels exist among these women. There is, however, one striking similarity: They understand the strength of their God. Their confidence in His ability to fight for them is reflected in their faces, their voices, and their words. Because these women know that God is strong enough for any battle they will face, they feel strong enough to face any battle.

Sue is one such woman. She told me about the day she hurried to get to her husband, who suffered from diabetes and had been taken to a hospital three hours away, in a fight for his life. It certainly wasn't her first crisis. After a painful childhood of almost unimaginable loss, she had endured a rape, the birth of a seriously disabled son, and two marriages to abusive men. Through it all, God had sustained and strengthened her, but she was tired.

Traveling was treacherous over the mountain pass that day as torrential sheets of Oregon rain made visibility nearly impossible. She turned the music up loud and let the sounds of worship wash over her weary soul. Suddenly a blue pickup truck began drifting into her lane, forcing her onto the shoulder of the road. She tried to veer around him, but her car tipped over and flipped several times, then skidded on its roof 120 feet before coming to a stop on the side of the mountain road. Witnesses would later say they were certain no one had survived. But Sue is most definitely a survivor.

As she sat, suspended upside down by her seat belt, wondering what the next seconds of her life would hold, she made a brave decision. Sue remembered the promise she had chosen years ago and quoted a thousand times . . . they were the words that had fastened her to sanity through the darkest times of life: "I can do all things through him who strengthens me" (Philippians 4:13).

All things. Sue had seen God show up when everyone else she loved had walked away. She had seen His footsteps on her battle-fields and had witnessed His supernatural strength. She knew He would show up this time too. Clinging tightly to the strength that comes from His Word, she began to say out loud all the things for which she was thankful. She thanked God that her car hadn't struck any other car. She thanked Him for the worship music she could still hear all around her. She thanked Him for whoever might come to get her out of that car. She just kept telling Him all the ways she knew He was strong enough for yet another messy moment.

Soon, someone did show up. Four people, all believers, worked to break the windows and cut her out of the car. Then they surrounded her on that rainy afternoon and prayed for peace and protection while they waited for help to arrive. Eventually, an ambulance came and Sue was taken to the hospital she had been en route to before the accident. She joined her husband there and rested once again in the strength of God.

The rest of Sue's story is filled with still more giants and more evidence of God's strength to overcome them. As we talked on a snowy day in a cozy coffee shop, I asked her how she had done it. One soldier to another, I needed to know how she had survived so many battles and come out so strong and beautiful. Tears streamed down her face as she tried to answer but had to stop when her voice caught with emotion. Finally, she lifted sparkling eyes for a breathtaking summation: "Oh, Bo," she said, "once we know how much He loves us, there's just nothing else."

There's just nothing else. When God comes to love us in our battle, our enemy is made weak and we are made strong. Even a villain like ALS, with the power to take the very breath from my beloved's lungs, is dwarfed and defeated by the strength, power, and "enoughness" of God. This knowledge makes our enemies cringe, but it should make us more confident and courageous than we have ever been.

THE ONLY COMPARING TO BE DONE

Here's a strong word of caution from my heart to yours: It's tempting to hold our giant up to the size of other people's giants, but this never helps. If our battle seems bigger than theirs, we can feel overwhelmed with fear or we may look to God and wonder why He hasn't loved us as well as He seems to love them. If our fight seems smaller, then we can fall into the trap of thinking we should be able to manage it without Him. Neither response is a good one. The only comparing that should be done is comparing your giant to your God. That comparison brings life and hope.

Battles of any size enable us to see the mighty arm of God and the power of His love for us. On the fighting field we see Him in action and experience the rewards of fighting in the shadow of

His supernatural strength. This, my friend, is treasure for the taking.

WORTH PONDERING

1. Journal about (or discuss with a friend) the enemies you are facing today. What is their size compared to the size of your God?
2. Read Psalm 18 out loud and list all the battle benefits that come from having God at the head of your fight.

WORTH DOING

Read Psalm 27 out loud and listen to the truth about the size of your God.

CHAPTER 5

What the Greeting Cards Won't Tell You

The Beauty of Endurance

A few years ago, right after our daughter Whitney got married, I spent the afternoon with her reading the many wonderful cards she had received from friends and family. They were pretty and sparkly, and each one wished her and her new husband something lovely. Some offered hope for joy, happiness, and prosperity. Some even wished them a house full of children (okay, maybe that one was mine!). But none mentioned the one thing that every couple absolutely *must* have in order to make a life together work. Not a single card said, "Wishing you the endurance you're going to need to stay married for fifty years."

While most of us understand that endurance is required for any marriage to go the distance, none of us wants to write it in a happy Hallmark card. The word *endurance* conjures up images of laborious longsuffering rather than hearts and rainbows. It makes marriage sound like a chore and a strain rather than heart-stopping romance. But with twenty-seven years of marriage under my belt, I can testify to the power of endurance over the power of rainbows, and I will stake my bets on the enduring couple over the swooning couple any day of the week. Endurance is not negative; it's one of the hidden treasures of the battlefield.

THE PERFECT PLACE TO GROW ENDURANCE

Few things create opportunities for growing endurance like time spent in battle, standing firm when we want to quit and holding our ground when it would be easier to punch the clock and call it a day. James wrote, "Consider it all joy, my brethren, when you encounter various trials, knowing that the testing of your faith produces endurance. And let endurance have its perfect result, so that you may be perfect and complete, lacking in nothing" (1:2-4, NASB).

Endurance is born from the testing of our faith, and the testing of our faith is the product of trials. Endurance is hard to develop off the battlefield because it is not so much a gift as it is a developed skill. Someone who spends long hours at the gym lifting weights would laugh at the idea that her sculpted muscles are a gift. She didn't get them by being in the right place at the right time or by paying large sums of money or by winning them in a poker game. Those muscles came through hard work. Not one day of hard work or two days, but day after day after day, building strength by lifting increasingly heavier weights and refusing to quit when the work got rough. That's endurance. We see this principle in David's life.

First Samuel 17 tells the story of his big win against Goliath, the Philistine's fiercest fighting machine. This is a fight for which

David volunteered, and then he ran in to meet that giant and cut off his head. So brave! If it were up to me, he would then have been able to rest and bask in his victory. However, when we travel down the road to chapter 18, we find that the hero became the hunted as King Saul's jealousy drove him to seek David's death by repeatedly putting him on the front lines against the Philistines.

Can you imagine facing the same enemy army day after day, simply because your boss is threatened by your success? I wonder how many mornings David wanted to pull the covers over his head and hide instead of fighting. I wonder if he was tempted to quit or run or go back to a safe, obscure life tending sheep. If so, he didn't give in. He didn't do any of those things. Instead, he showed up and fought and won. Though Saul had hoped the Philistines would kill David, the strategy backfired horribly. All that time on the battlefield increased David's skill, strength, and reputation, so much so that the people sang, "Saul has killed his thousands, but David his tens of thousands" (1 Samuel 18:7, HCSB).

Turns out the very thing that Saul had planned to use to destroy David, God used to build endurance in him and to prepare him for the enemies he would face when he became king. In fact, David's endurance training had really started years earlier, in a lonely field when the young shepherd killed a lion and a bear. Every battle became practice for the next one. Each trial that he faced head-on, without wavering or giving up, produced a store-house of endurance that he would draw from in battles down the road.

I've seen this same principle working in my life. I am discovering that I'm not as frail as I thought I was. You see, I've never been very resilient. Some mornings I've wanted to give up over battles as big as No Cream for My Coffee. This throw-in-the-towel tendency of mine does not bode well for my success in a battle with a giant the size of ALS. However, it turns out that all the battles I have fought leading up to this one have built endurance that I didn't even realize I had. I never wanted to grow endurance; it's just the fortunate result of having survived some previous fights.

Here's an example. For a full year before his diagnosis, Steve had a job that required him to spend well over half his time in Florida. If you're curious, Orlando, Florida, is 2,906 miles and three time zones from Bend, Oregon. During that year Steve missed three kids' birthdays, our twenty-fifth anniversary, and about half of all the garbage days (I'm not gifted at remembering garbage day). That year I learned to shovel snowy sidewalks, scrape my own windshield, and play basketball in the driveway with our son. I learned to sit in church alone and go to sleep alone and drink coffee in the mornings alone. That season was a battle in so many ways, but I am now drawing from the endurance I built up in that fight. There was no way I could have known how much work was happening inside of me through a situation I would have so happily escaped had the option presented itself.

GETTING BACK UP

The truth is, if we lack the endurance to see a battle through to the end, it won't matter much if we are strong or have the skill we need to do battle. Plenty of men and women have given up on marriage or parenting or a job simply because they didn't have the endurance to go the distance. Some have started over with new families only to find that eventually the going will always get tough. Endurance will inevitably be required to achieve anything of value. That's why we should be thankful for our battlefields.

My sweet cousin Michelle knows the beauty of endurance born out of battles. She waited a long time to find the man of her dreams. Not long after Kirk swept her off her feet, they married and were soon expecting their first child. A miscarriage early on left them sad, but not disheartened. A positive pregnancy test a few months later was the good news they were hoping for, and they happily started preparing for their baby's autumn arrival. Shortly after celebrating the pregnancy, Michelle was devastated to learn that her mother, Jean, had been diagnosed with fast-moving pancreatic cancer.

Despite the grim prognosis, Michelle's fervent prayer was that her mom would get to hold the baby before she died. Jean tried to hang on. She prayed for healing and thanked God for every day that He gave her. However, just a few weeks after the diagnosis, Jean lost her fight with cancer and went to be with Jesus. It all happened so quickly that it was hard for the family to absorb and accept.

As they went about preparing for Jean's funeral, Michelle began having some sporadic contractions. She chalked it up to stress until she awoke in the early morning and realized the contractions were very steady at ten minutes apart. Her doctor suggested they come in to the hospital as a precaution, but Michelle still wasn't worried that the situation was serious. After trying three times to find the baby's heartbeat, a nurse called for the doctor, who confirmed the worst: There were no signs of life.

The next morning, Michelle gave birth to a stillborn baby girl they named Layla. They held her little body, took pictures for scrapbooks, and then did something really beautiful. Because of the timing of the two deaths, just days apart, they tucked that little darling in with her grandmother, and their frail earthly bodies were laid to rest together. On a sunny, sad Saturday in June, Michelle attended the funeral for her daughter and her mother. Sorrow upon sorrow.

In the months that followed, Michelle navigated the brutal terrain of the battlefield of grief. She asked a lot of questions of doctors about what had gone wrong with her pregnancies, and she asked some tough questions of God. It felt like she hadn't just lost a mother and a daughter; she had also lost a long-lived and deeply held dream of becoming a mom. She wondered if she could risk heartache again or if it might be best to just pack that dream away. Ultimately, she says, she wrestled those questions into a place of submission to the will of her Father. She chose to find comfort in His Word, stand in faith, and try again. She would trust His goodness and let endurance lead to hope.

Because of this battle Michelle became stronger and more confident in who God is and in His love for her. She was knocked down by suffering, but she got back up and believed, and is now walking prayerfully through her third pregnancy, believing that she will be a mom this Christmas. Michelle has endured much in a short time, but she is stronger than ever and ready to face the future with faith.

IF YOU SEE AN ESCAPE ROUTE

All battles come packaged with a certain amount of pain, suffering, sorrow, hardship, or anxiety. Some, like physical illness, have no clear escape route, and the only option is to endure. Others, like battles on the job or in relationships, may offer compelling off-ramps. Sometimes the wise option is to leave, as was the case for my friend Linda who was in an abusive marriage. Other times, however, it's hard to know whether to skip out or stick it out. When that is the case it helps to ask ourselves, What is on the other side if I endure? Will I grow and be better for it? When it's not possible to predict the outcome, pray and ask. Let the Holy Spirit guide you in this.

Jesus, when faced with the most intense battle in all of history, death on the cross, asked His Father if there was any other way.[1] But, ultimately, He submitted to the will of God, and Hebrews 12 gives us a look into His motivation: "For the joy that was set before him [He] endured the cross, despising the shame" (verse 2). Love led Jesus to the cross; obedience and endurance held Him there. I'm so grateful that He chose to stay, to outlast the suffering, to endure it all for you and me.

FAR-REACHING REWARDS

As we've seen, our time on the battlefield helps us develop endurance for the long haul. But one of the beautiful, hidden treasures of endurance is that it makes us a valuable resource for others who are entering a Really Big Battle.

I recently sat in a room full of lovely young mothers and several moms-to-be. The conversation was alive with labor and delivery stories as the experienced women offered advice and encouragement to the expectant first-timers. The prevailing theme from every one of those wise women was this: It's hard, but it's so worth it. Not one of them said, "I sure hope you survive labor, sister. Maybe you should just quit the pregnancy right now." Instead, they drew from their memories to lend their endurance experiences to those coming after them. I see the same dynamic in the marriage class that meets every week at our church. Those leading the class have faced seemingly insurmountable odds in their own marriages, and their experience on that battlefield serves as life support for couples who are deciding whether or not endurance is worth it.

Another reward of endurance is joy. We'll talk more about this in chapter 7, but I have to mention it here because joy is so closely connected to endurance. I love Romans 5:3-5 because these verses read like a line of falling dominoes, one good thing leading to the next: "We rejoice in our sufferings, knowing that suffering produces endurance, and endurance produces character, and character produces hope, and hope does not put us to shame." The process of suffering and standing and sticking it out is leading somewhere good; it's leading to joy. That's happy news!

When I was in labor with my first child, I remember a moment after two hours of pushing when the pain was so relentless that I decided I no longer wanted to be a participant in the process. As soon as I got a break between contractions, I looked earnestly at my doctor and said, "I would like to go home now please." He smiled at me sympathetically, but instead of telling me I was crazy (thank you, Dr. Harvey!), he said, "Remember why you're doing this. You're about to meet your baby."

I still wasn't convinced I wanted to stick it out, but it helped to be reminded about what was on the other side of the fight for new life. I've been in labor three times since, and each time I reached a similar point of exhaustion and frustration with the pain, but I never again asked to go home before the baby came. I never even entertained the idea. Two things had changed in me: (1) I had built up endurance. Because I had survived the pain once, I was certain I could do it again. This gave me hope and strength that I didn't have the first time around. Experience teaches us how to endure. (2) I had a beautiful little girl (and then two, and then three) as proof that the pain would lead to joy. I knew it would be hard, but enduring the pain was the only way to get to the teeny tiny feet and the cute button nose.

As you face your battle today, I wish you hope. And health and life and, if possible, a quick resolution that allows you to move into peaceful country. But I also wish you increasing measures of endurance that enable you to survive and thrive on this battlefield and all that are to come. Maybe the world will begin to value endurance for the prize that it is and Hallmark will make an appropriate greeting card. Until then, just know that I'm wishing it for you.

WORTH PONDERING

1. What is the most difficult thing you have ever endured?
2. How did it affect you?
3. Can you think of a time when you gave up rather than stuck it out? How might things be different today if you had stuck it out?

WORTH DOING

Write out Romans 5:3-5 in three different translations (you can find many translations online). Circle the words that mean the most to you and put that paper somewhere you will see it every day.

CHAPTER 6

Wearing the Glasses of God

The Beauty of Eternal Perspective

My daughter Tess is a great photographer. She's young, but she's already built an active business capturing the big moments of people's lives. I love this passion of hers because it has given her so many opportunities to focus her energy, and it has taught her how to prioritize. The latter skill is a necessity in photography because . . . well, have you seen the price of equipment lately? An arm and a leg. Wanting to keep all her limbs, Tess once even took back the dress she had just purchased for homecoming and instead used the money for a new zoom lens. That, by the way, turned out to be a brilliant decision from nearly every angle.

The right equipment makes a difference in the quality of Tess's photos, but the cost of her gear is not the primary strength of her skill. How do I know this? Because I have taken photos with her camera and no one would pay a single dime for them. Tess's gift is not the gift of a good Nikon; it's the gift of *perspective*. She sees the world from an angle that many people miss. It's not unusual to find her on the ground, pointing her camera up at a tree rather than centering it in the middle of the frame straight on, like I would. While I would shoot a whole flower, Tess shoots one petal or a dew drop on the leaf. I might shoot a photo of an entire bench. She shoots the patch of paint as it peels away from the splintering wood. Tess loves to find the hidden charm and blow it up big, making it the star of the photo, sometimes even making us wonder what it is we're looking at. It's a gift I adore because she helps us see beauty in our world that we would otherwise step right over.

Time on the battlefield has a way of shifting our perspective. Perspective helps us reevaluate events and emotions so that we can better understand their significance. Sometimes, perspective means the small things become big; other times it means the big things become small. Perspective adjusts the lenses through which we view the world, ourselves, and our God, and this can be good or bad when we are in the middle of a big fight.

WHY PERSPECTIVE MATTERS

A remarkable example of the power of perspective is found in Numbers 13. Here we find the children of Israel, camped just on the edge of the Promised Land, Canaan. God has promised to give them the whole place, but there are a few strings attached. Specifically, an entire people group and an unsettling number of giants. If there's one big truth the Israelites packed with them out of Egypt, it's that whoever possesses the property possesses the power. They know that in order to end this season as desert dwellers, they'll have to roll up their sleeves and fight.

God, who certainly knew the challenges the Israelites were about to face, wanted them to understand that this prize was worth fighting for, so He told them to send some scouts ahead to take a look around. Moses chose one man from each tribe. I love that the spies are listed by name. Shammua. Shaphat. Caleb. Igal. Joshua. Palti. Gaddiel. Gaddi. Ammiel. Sethur. Nahbi. Geuel. Names help us know that these guys were real — *real* men with *real* families, dreams, and desires. They and the rest of the Israelites had known generations of slavery and just two short years of freedom (during which God had shown His love for them by dealing breathtaking blows to their enemies). Their eyes had watched the walls of the Red Sea roll back, water pour out of rocks, and food fall from the sky.[1] They were accustomed to having a supernatural compass overhead night and day,[2] showing them exactly when to stop or go. God was using this two-year season in these twelve lives to shift these men's perspectives from that of slaves to that of sons. Now He was ready to show them that this beautiful country was ripe for the taking.

Twelve men went out and explored the land for forty days, and they came back loaded down with its fruit: grapes and pomegranates and figs the size of fists. (Actually, I don't know how big the figs were, but it makes a good story — and we do know the fruit was really big!) All twelve agreed that the land was stunning and inviting, but they also agreed on something else: The Canaanites were strong and intimidating. Uh-oh. Dream deterrent. When they heard this news, the people were concerned, but Caleb stepped up and reassured them, "Let us go up at once and occupy it, for we are well able to overcome it" (Numbers 13:30).

Ten of them, however, had a different perspective. "We are not able to go up against the people, for they are stronger than we are" (verse 31). And look at this amazing, awful admission: "We seemed to ourselves like grasshoppers, and so we seemed to them" (verse 33). Oh dear. When we begin adopting the perspective of our enemy, we are in really big trouble.

Satan will always use our circumstances to break us down; God wants to use those same circumstances to grow us up and into an eternal perspective. And sometimes, Satan has very little work to do because we are already inclined to believe that we are grasshoppers. All he has to do is agree with us. If you regularly say things about yourself that you would never say about someone else ("I'm so stupid . . . so overweight . . . so ugly . . . so weak"), please stop. Stop immediately. Stop doing your enemy's work for him. Start seeing your life, your abilities, and your future from God's perspective.

Back to our story. The twelve spies agreed on nearly everything. They agreed that the land was a treasure and that the opposition was large. However, two of the men parted company with the others in their perspective. The other ten viewed the battle from their own perspective, but Joshua and Caleb viewed it from God's perspective. They realized that their ability to win or lose had nothing to do with their opponent, and everything to do with what God wanted for them. God had led them into this battle, and He had assured them of victory.

> Joshua the son of Nun and Caleb the son of Jephunneh . . . tore their clothes and said to all the congregation of the people of Israel, "The land, which we passed through to spy it out, is an exceedingly good land. If the Lord delights in us, he will bring us into this land and give it to us, a land that flows with milk and honey. Only do not rebel against the Lord. And do not fear the people of the land, for they are bread for us. Their protection is removed from them, and the Lord is with us; do not fear them." (Numbers 14:6-9)

These words from two brave men leave me breathless every time I read them. This was not just a display of courage against a distant, unknown enemy; Joshua and Caleb were standing their ground in the face of an angry mob of *friends*. God Himself had to show up to stop the crowd from stoning them.

Sometimes having the correct perspective is not a big crowd-pleaser, but it is always, *always* a great God-pleaser. In the end, Joshua and Caleb were the only spies allowed to enter the Promised Land, and this after spending forty years circling it. The other ten spies — Shammua, Shaphat, Igal, Palti, Gaddiel, Gaddi, Ammiel, Sethur, Nahbi, Geuel — ended their lives in wilderness graves, no longer slaves but never quite sons.

This story is a stunning illustration of why perspective is so important: It can take us to the doorstep of our dreams, or it can keep us retracing our old footsteps, year after miserable year, falling for the same dumb tricks, hiding from the same old enemy, and never experiencing the life we long for. The difference between winning and losing — for at least ten men and all those who listened to them — was their perspective. Seriously, go back and read those names out loud again. Even though they had been promised dream homes in a beautiful land, real men died real deaths in the wilderness because their earthbound perspective kept them out of their inheritance.

MY CRASH COURSE IN PERSPECTIVE

This season of battle has been a crash course in perspective and has helped me answer the questions about what really matters in life and distinguish between the things that are bad, good, and best. Almost overnight, I felt that I had been pulled up into God's lap and invited to see my world through His lens. Let me tell you, from that angle, my view of nearly everything has changed. Here are just a few examples:

Money

I have always struggled to have faith for finances. I can see many seasons in my life when my perspective on money kept me from fulfilling the things God had for me. Enter a terminal diagnosis that not only sends our family's primary breadwinner into retirement fifteen years early but also contains a file of medical bills so fat that we hide it lest our kids see it and give up on their dreams for higher education.

However, the strangest thing happened when we looked up into the eyeballs of the ALS enemy: The money didn't matter much. We were able to see that the bills and the current economy and Steve's lack of a paycheck are actually small players in a much bigger battle. Our fight is not going to be with dollars and cents; it is with our ability to trust God to provide for our needs.

We didn't gain this eternal perspective overnight, but we did come to it fairly quickly as Steve and I made the unified decision that our vision would be focused on God, who fights for us. If He is with us in this battle—and we know He is—then He is in charge of both the victory and the price of the victory. When worry wants to wedge its sneaky foot in the door of my peace, I sometimes have to remind myself of our decision to focus on God, but overall I am overwhelmed at the way the Holy Spirit has helped realign our view on faith and finances through this fight. No matter how the win looks in the end, this is one of the beautiful treasures I will carry off this battlefield.

I don't know the amount of what is or isn't in your checkbook today. I do, however, know the power of your God. You will find that amazing peace accompanies a perspective that is freshly focused on His strength.

The Size of Other People's Battles

The first time we met with our ALS advocate, we talked about the strong emotional reactions we get when we say that Steve is fighting Lou Gehrig's disease. He smiled sadly and said, "Yep. This is one of the only diagnoses where you're really hoping for a brain tumor instead." (If I had a dollar for every time I've heard, "This is nothing compared to what you're going through . . ." I wouldn't need a fresh perspective on finances.) However, Steve and I don't feel that our battle is worse than what other people face. We know this disease is rotten, but we have each other. Our kids are healthy. We are not controlled by substances, fear, or frustration. We are convinced that our battle has great purpose and that we are being used by a big God to help bring hope to a broken world.

My heart breaks when I see people who have all their strength and yet seem to have found no opportunities for investing it into anything with lasting meaning. Some couples will be gifted with a fifty-year marriage without enjoying a moment of it. Many people will live long, healthy lives, but they're so broken by rejection that, unless they experience a perspective shift, they will live out their days never knowing what it means to be truly loved. Oh, friends, the intensity of this battle has pushed one essential truth to the surface of my heart: My life is still abundantly blessed. And that point of view keeps me soft and compassionate and moving forward. It keeps me looking for ways to help people find meaning and hope in a world that offers so little of either. Perspective is powerful.

What I Really Have

One night in church while Steve was out of town, our pastor opened the service by having us pray with each other. He said, "Perhaps you're facing an issue with your health or a crisis in your finances, or maybe you just have a lot of anxiety about your future." I was three for three. I bet you know what I'm talking about, because I bet you have faced a similar moment. Most battles bleed into several areas of life, and it's easy to feel like everything is being shaken or taken. On this particular night, I was swimming in an ocean of fear, certain that my tightly woven life was coming unraveled. Somewhere in the back of my mind, though, I knew that couldn't be true. All I could do was beg God to break through the tumult and let me see from His perspective.

After a long night of tossing and turning, I woke up the next morning with a list forming in my head. It was almost like a far-off drumbeat, percolating in my spirit and pushing its way to my cognitive thinking. It was not my own clever creating but the grace of God showing up at just the right moment with just the right words. I sat down with my computer and started writing as a new perspective flowed out onto the page. Just twenty-four hours earlier, I could not see beyond what I was losing. Now, the fog had cleared and my new vantage point gave me a clear view of the things that still remained.

- I have salvation (see Ephesians 1:7).
- I have a beautiful and eternal inheritance (see Psalm 16:6).
- I have been given a spirit of love, power, and safe thinking, so I will not fear (see 2 Timothy 1:7).
- I have a healthy understanding of His Word, of truth, and of His love for me. I can use this to create order, rest, and power in my internal and external world.
- I have a mind that is being renewed and transformed by the power of Christ (see Romans 12:2).
- I have a healthy, whole physical body.
- I have relationships that bring joy, safety, unity, and

wholeness to my life. (Here I listed all the names of
people who are dear to me.)

- I have access to joy — in seasons, in laughter, in worship,
in conversations, in hope, in love, and in relationships. I
also have sorrow because of the great joy I have been
given. Sorrow serves as the reminder that God has
blessed me abundantly with things I want to hold on to
forever, and it also points my focus back to heaven,
where all blessing will be mine to keep (see Isaiah
61:1-3).

Wow. My *Have Nots* list, though still daunting, didn't look
like much competition next to this bountiful stream of mercy
and grace. In the days and weeks that followed, this new perspective on the *I Haves* became a wellspring for me. I read my list
first thing each morning and again at night before falling asleep,
and I ran to it every time I felt fear or confusion or grief trying
to swallow me up. I read it for comfort and clarity. I printed it
out and put copies in strategic locations throughout my house
and in my office and in my car. Before long, I needed the list
less and less because I was able to recall it from memory. Our
fight has woven this beautiful perspective into the fabric of
my life.

Now, when a fiery dart of a thought comes flying in that says,
"You're losing everything," my default response is, "Nope. I have
a beautiful and eternal inheritance. I have relationships that bring
life. I have joy. My problems may seem large in size, but they are
finite in number. His blessings for me, on the other hand, are
enormous, eternal, and infinite." This list has been true of me for
decades, but it's only this season on the battlefield that brought it
to the surface where I could actually focus on it, memorize it, and
live it.

Sometimes I think the war gets so long and so fierce that we begin to wonder if there's even anything left worth fighting for. Taking stock of what you know you have will bring perspective to your season and enable you to clearly see His gifts, even in the midst of very real suffering.

Time

Most of my life I have been one of those annoying people who watches TV while reading a book or surfing the Internet or playing a game on my phone. If my family isn't at the dinner table with me, I do research on my computer while I eat. When I talk on the phone, I do the dishes or sort through the mail. Something about this frenetic mental movement makes me feel productive, even though it's actually counterproductive. I often found that when I retraced my footsteps at the end of the day, I could say that I had been busy but hadn't done much of anything. That's really sad. I didn't ever mean to live that way; I just fell into a common trap called I Have All the Time in the World.

This battle has adjusted my perspective on time. I no longer see time as a limitless commodity but rather like money in a bank account that I must spend wisely and make count. Ironically, this perspective has not sped me up; it has slowed me down. It makes me more intentional about all the decisions I make with the 1,440 minutes in my day. It causes me to really look at and listen to my husband and children . . . to absorb their beauty and wit and to recognize the way that God is shaping their lives. It helps me enjoy a good meal without distraction and absorb the intricacies of a brilliant sunset with my beloved, understanding that I won't get that moment back again. This change is bigger than just feeling as if I need to stockpile these memory-making minutes with Steve; it applies to every area of my life. I'm learning to live each day and love what God puts inside of it for me to enjoy or to accomplish. In fact, this shift in perspective is also making the process of writing this book exhilarating rather than exhausting. I love this change in the way I track time, and I'm thankful every day for this piece of beauty from the battle.

A BIG AND BEAUTIFUL LAND
FOR THE TAKING

These are just four examples of the countless ways this battlefield is aligning and adjusting my perspective. I could also mention that I'm not as afraid of taking risks as I used to be, and neither is my husband. Steve's new favorite line when faced with a dangerous opportunity is "Well, what do I have to lose?" and he's only partially kidding. Satan wants to use this sickness to push us into a corner and get us to believe that God cannot protect us or to make us so focused on our battle that we have no compassion or courage to give to others. He would love to see me immobilized by thoughts of what our life might look like financially if I become a single mom.

These are big giants, yes, but — hear this truth well — *there is a big and beautiful land for the taking!* It's the land where God's love prevails in every circumstance. It's the place where spirits soar and hope rises regardless of the condition of our bodies or the state of our economy. Where He leads us, He will feed us and will deal with our enemies.

Steve. Bo. Whitney. Corey. Tess. Victoria. Josiah. These are the real names of the real people who are beginning to understand that their God is bigger than their giants, and they *will* build dream homes in the Promised Land.

No matter what you're facing today, your ability to win the

battle will be closely connected, if not completely intertwined, with your perspective. Perhaps you feel that your circumstances have pushed you down until you have no more strength to stand. That's okay. Flowers are still flowers whether they're viewed straight through the camera lens or from flat on the ground, looking up. Ask God to show you a new angle on your fight, on your foe, and on your future. Be willing to let Him pull you up to His altitude so He can show you the world from there. It's a great view because He is a great God.

If you are in the middle of a Really Big Battle today, especially if it's gone on for a while, I think you're going to like where we're headed next. Or if you are weary and wondering whether to stick it out on the battlefield, this next discovery is for you.

WORTH PONDERING

1. What is the land that God has promised you? (Think big!)
2. In spite of the size of the giants, what is your current perspective on the size, strength, and goodness of your God? (Think bigger!)
3. Are there some perspective adjustments you could make to help you face your fight with faith?

WORTH DOING

Take an hour in a quiet place and write your story out in third person (as if you're a stranger, looking at your battle from the outside). Write honestly, and then ask yourself this question: Are there other perspectives—positive or negative—from which this story could be seen? If you were to adopt the most positive perspective, how would it change the way you fight, the way you rest, and the way you trust?

CHAPTER 7

An Unlikely Dance

The Beauty of Joy and Sorrow

My sisters and I once took a road trip from Oregon to Montana, but we were diverted when two of us ended up in an emergency room in Ritzville, Washington, with the kind of food poisoning that makes you wish you had never been born. To this day, that trip remains the gold standard for what it means to be truly sick. "I'm sick," I'll tell my sister on the phone, "but I'm not *Ritzville* sick."

Some experiences pack such a hefty emotional punch that they alter the way we feel and see life long after the initial sting is over. I remember the day that we sat in our doctor's office at Providence Hospital as she told us that Steve's muscle test had changed, and he now met the criteria for ALS. I remember looking out her window at the Portland streets that I have always loved, wondering how I would ever love them again. As I went to the waiting room to tell my parents the results, I wondered how I would stay upright. I buried my head in Steve's chest and sobbed as my dad and mom hugged us and pleaded with God to come into our mourning and turn it into something beautiful. In the spinning, swirling thoughts of that day, I knew God was with us and I knew He would carry us, but I wondered how I would ever feel joy again. I could imagine getting through a day without crying, but I could not conjure up any scenario where sorrow did not win out over joy.

Sorrow seems very bossy to me. It's a brawny, bully emotion that squeezes the air out of lighter, loftier feelings like happiness and cheer. And if the nature of the battle we face brings sorrow with it (which nearly all battles do), it can seem that even if we survive the sorrow, it will still leave a permanent mark on our joy.

When I first walked onto the battlefield of ALS, I couldn't imagine joyful moments in our future, and I couldn't even fully enjoy the good memories from the past. My heart was trapped beneath the weight of grief, and I thought I would never take a full, deep breath of joy again. I was wrong.

THE DINNER THAT OPENED THE DOOR TO JOY

Two days after we returned home from that fateful doctor visit, Steve took our son out to dinner. Josiah had known that his dad was sick, but we had been deliberately vague about the details until we knew what we were facing. We didn't want him to have to carry an unnecessary weight on his eleven-year-old shoulders. Finally it was time to tell him the whole story, and we knew that this moment would mark his future. I halfheartedly offered to go along, but Steve wanted to tell Josiah without me being present, and I was so relieved. I would have instinctively tried to fix things, and this situation could not be fixed; it could only be shared and then shifted to the shoulders of Jesus. I had no doubt that Steve would do a fantastic job with his son, but it's never been harder for me to see my two men leave our house.

While they were gone, I paced and prayed and paced and prayed. I worried my words up to Jesus and wrung my hands until I finally texted Steve and asked him to please let me know as soon as he knew that our boy was okay. Finally, the text came back: "We talked, we cried, and then Joe said, 'Can I have another breadstick?'" Oh, I loved and will forever cherish the memory of that text. My husband knew exactly how to tell me that our son was down but not out, pressed but not crushed. And I longed to know the kind of childlike simplicity that can truly mourn a terminal diagnosis, but still really enjoy a good breadstick.

During that dinner, Steve asked Josiah a very important question. He said, "What is the one thing you would love for us to do together this year?" Josiah thought about it and decided that he would like to go to an Indianapolis Colts game, and then they talked about how fun that would be and how they might make it happen. That conversation was a lightbulb moment for Steve, and it led to similar conversations with the rest of our children. Each one picked a dream trip with their dad, and then we set to work to make it happen.

Though it seemed impossible at the time, God added His supernatural resources to our dreaming and provided all that we needed to live out each of these amazing experiences with our kids while Steve was still able. Exactly one year after the diagnosis, we had marked all four off the list. We had driven an RV through Yellowstone and stopped to let the buffalo cross the road, Tess's camera shutter clicking nearly nonstop. We had climbed the steps of the Colosseum in Rome and eaten churros and chocolate in Spain. We had soaked in the sun in Florida and then basked in the beauty of a concert by Andrea Bocelli. And Josiah ate nachos in the Lucas Oil Stadium, wearing his Peyton Manning jersey, cheering on the Colts with his dad by his side. Though we had rarely taken even one vacation in a year's time, in this incredible year we managed four. We have enough photos to fill many albums and enough memories for a lifetime.

In the beginning of our whirlwind trip-taking, I found myself caught in a tangled ball of emotions. I wanted to delight in these beautiful moments with our kids, but Steve's condition created a dark backdrop of sorrow. Everything I would have otherwise been excited about was filtered through the sights and sounds of our battle. As much as I wanted to enjoy these once-in-a-lifetime experiences, sorrow kept pressing in and nudging joy just out of reach. Finally, I was exhausted by the internal tug-of-war and asked God to help me find His perspective on how to love our life while still grieving the potential loss. I don't know why it takes me so long to throw up my hands and tell Him I'm not going to be able to muscle my way through it, but I'm always so glad when I finally turn to Him for fresh answers and new strength.

The idea of letting in some real, true joy began warming my sad heart like sunlight streaming through an open window on a winter's day. I started to embrace the happy moments for what they could bring into my life without letting the sad moments steal away their beauty. At first I almost felt guilty, like the little kid who laughs inappropriately at a funeral. But as I pointed out earlier, I am discovering through the Word and through experience that joy and sorrow are not mutually exclusive emotions. Both are hidden treasures found on the battlefield.

THE OIL THAT SOFTENS THE SUFFERING

I used to think that sorrow eradicated all joy. When I had a happy day, I feared watching the evening news because I knew that some story of murder or mayhem would make me sad and — bam! — good-bye joy. The Bible, however, does not support this idea. Instead, it insists that joy and sorrow can comingle in lovely ways, bringing balance to life and hope to our hurting.

The apostle Paul made these strong declarations in his letter to the Philippians:

Rejoice in the Lord always; again I will say, rejoice. (Philippians 4:4)

For his sake I have suffered the loss of all things and count them as rubbish, in order that I may gain Christ and be found in him, not having a righteousness of my own that comes from the law, but that which comes through faith in Christ, the righteousness from God that depends on faith — that I may know him and the power of his resurrection, and may share his sufferings, becoming like him in his death. (Philippians 3:8-10)

Paul understood that both joy and suffering are important. My vantage point allows me to see that joy makes the suffering possible, and that suffering makes the joy more beautiful.

The pain of my battlefield has served as a spotlight on the things in my life that are truly lovely. I am learning to embrace the wonder of the colors of fall and the sounds of my family around the dinner table. I am breathing in deeply the smell of Baby Magic on my grandson's freshly washed skin and delighting in the fact that he has his grandpa's eyes. I am treasuring every cup of coffee I share with a friend while telling each other stories. These moments of pure joy must be lived fully because they are the oil that softens the suffering. Joy that shows up in the heat of battle is one of the most beautiful things I have ever known. I'm so glad I stopped believing it was impossible.

THE BLESSING OF SORROW

I've never had to convince anyone that joy is good, but sorrow is a tougher sell. Sometimes we Christians describe a life following Jesus as something straight out of the pages of a pretty magazine. The house is beautiful, the kids have clean faces and matching socks, the refrigerator is full. We confuse the favor of God with the benefits of living in a blessed country during an era of relative prosperity. However, the words of Jesus Himself, "In this world you will have trouble" (John 16:33, NIV), defy the idea of a picture-perfect existence in our preeternal world.

The Bible doesn't run from sorrow but rather encourages us to see it as one of the blessings born on the battlefield. I have experienced at least three distinctly beautiful benefits from sorrow.

Sorrow connects us to the comfort of God's presence.

The Sermon on the Mount is Jesus' most extensive monologue and is the best foundation we have on which to build a theology about the blessing and favor of God. In it, He mentions eight specific "blessings," including poverty, hunger, and persecution. One has grown near and dear to my heart: "Blessed are those who mourn, for they shall be comforted" (Matthew 5:4).

I realize that comfort seems like a cheap consolation prize for mourning. It's like, "Blessed are those who break their arm, for they shall get a shiny new cast!" This promise, however, is so much bigger and better than that.

The Greek word for comfort is the word *parakaleo*. It's formed from two words: *para*, which means "close or near," and *kaleo*, which means "to call, invite, invoke, or beseech."[1] Blessed are those who mourn, for they shall be invited to come near. God's beautiful, intimate presence is the blessing in our sorrow. When we are suffering, He comes near. He calls us near. He draws us out of our hurting and into His healing. It's not just because we need to be with Him, it's also because He loves to be with us. Here's another verse just to prove it:

> The Lord [earnestly] waits [expecting, looking, and longing] to be gracious to you; and therefore He lifts Himself up, that He may have mercy on you and show loving-kindness to you. For the Lord is a God of justice. Blessed (happy, fortunate, to be envied) are all those who [earnestly] wait for Him, who expect and look and long for Him [for His victory, His favor, His love, His peace, His joy, and His matchless, unbroken companionship]! (Isaiah 30:18, AMP)

Every time I read that verse, I picture the Lord earnestly waiting. I can see Him searching for a chance to meet with me, hoping that I will turn to Him, run to Him, and sit in His arms without squirming away. I find myself *longing* for the gift of His matchless, unbroken companionship and wondering how I can find that in my life. Well, the next verse tells the whole story, and the story matches the words of Jesus' sermon perfectly:

> O people who dwell in Zion at Jerusalem, you will weep no more. He will surely be gracious to you *at the sound of your cry*; when He hears it, He will answer you. And though the Lord gives you the bread of adversity and the water of affliction, yet your Teacher *will not hide Himself any more*, but your eyes will constantly behold your Teacher. (verses 19-20, AMP, emphasis added)

God is gracious to us at the sound of our weeping. He uses adversity and affliction to draw us to Himself and to reveal Himself to us in ways we have not seen before. God's comforting presence is an extravagant reward, one that we can undervalue . . . until we are in the heat of a battle.

That was certainly true for me. I had never asked for suffering so that I could experience His comfort. I hate to cry. *Hate it*. Yet in the past months I have spent more time immersed in the murky waters of weeping than I have in all my previous days combined. In the beginning, when sadness pushed tears to the surface, I beat them down. I excelled at distracting myself by changing my thoughts as frantically as possible or by trying to Bible-verse my way out of the pain. It works for a bit, and then — eventually — the waves cannot be held at bay and the crying just comes. I have abandoned my old method.

Now when the battle gets hot and sorrow overwhelms me, I hear in my heart the word *parakaleo*. God is near to the broken-hearted, and my tears are bringing me near to His healing. Weeping has become a supernatural tether that draws me back to the arms of the only One who can give the comfort I need. I can try to gut it out on my own, or I can let sorrow usher me right into the presence of Jesus.

Sorrow connects us to the heart of Jesus for His world.

When I was little, my Sunday school teacher challenged the class to memorize a verse in the Bible, so I chose the shortest one: "Jesus wept" (John 11:35). Though I committed these two words to memory, I had no clue as to the depth of their meaning until I was much older. The story is this: Jesus' friends Mary and Martha had lost their brother, Lazarus, to a sudden illness. They had sent Jesus a message before Lazarus died, but Jesus had chosen to stay where He was rather than go to them. When He did arrive, Lazarus had been in the tomb for four days and the sisters were mourning their loss. Though Jesus knew that Lazarus's condition was temporary, He was not numb to the grief of those around Him. John painted a beautifully emotive picture of the scene: "When Jesus saw her weeping, and the Jews who had come with her also weeping, he was deeply moved in his spirit and greatly troubled. And he said, 'Where have you laid him?' They said to him, 'Lord, come and see.' Jesus wept" (11:33-35).

Jesus wept because His friends wept. He felt what they felt. He felt the sting of sorrow because He loved them. Let this one stunning truth wrap around your heart like a soft blanket on a cool evening: Jesus weeps with you. The One who created the concept of emotion does not live in a state of anesthetized indifference. He hurts for the hurting.

Here's another astonishing encounter from the pen of Mark:

> They brought to him a man who was deaf and had a speech impediment, and they begged him to lay his hand on him. And taking him aside from the crowd privately, he put his fingers into his ears, and after spitting touched his tongue. And looking up to heaven, he sighed and said to him, "Ephphatha," that is, "Be opened." (7:32-34)

This passage doesn't tell us Jesus wept; it tells us He sighed. Sighing doesn't sound dramatic, but the Greek word in this verse is *stenazo*, and it means "to grieve and groan."[2] Even though Jesus was going to heal the deaf man, that didn't stop Him from sharing in the man's suffering.

In Mark 3 Jesus healed a man with a withered hand. He grieved over the hardness of the onlookers' hearts. I'm telling you, Jesus feels deeply for us. He feels sadness with us and for us. Sorrow led Him to lay His life down for us. When we experience sorrow, it helps us understand His heart for the world that lies trapped beneath the sway of the heartache of sin.[3]

When we taste sorrow's tears, we become more like Jesus by learning to share in His suffering. If we'll let it, sorrow can keep our hearts connected to His heart of compassion for our world.

This is a great gift from the battlefield because it makes us effective, capable colaborers in the kingdom, and it brings purpose to our pain.

Sorrow connects us to the hearts of those who suffer.

My friend Sue, whom I told you about in chapter 4, is sought after as a mentor by the women in our church and in our city. People turn to her and trust her with their story, not because she's a well-known author or speaker, but because they know she's been there. Talking to her, they feel the depth of her empathy; she understands suffering. She doesn't minimize sorrow; neither does she allow for it to be the end of the road. Sue encourages women in a fierce fight to find the beauty, become more like Jesus, and then turn to help someone else. That women trust and turn to her is one of the greatest joys of her life, and it is a direct result of the battles she has faced and fought with faith. The sorrow she has experienced has qualified her in a unique way for the joy of walking in her calling.

Do you have a heart to help the hurting? Don't be surprised by sorrow. Sorrow in our own battles enables us to experience a new compassion for others in battle, and this makes us more like Jesus. It molds us into more effective ministers of the gospel, and I believe that the inevitable result will be a whole new level of joy.

Are you seeing the delicate dance that takes place between sorrow and joy? It's beautiful, and it produces deep, divine things in us that just can't happen another way. Again I'll reiterate that God does not cause sorrow, but He is brilliant at using it to create a perfect work in us because He loves us just that much.

Very shortly you will move from part 1 to part 2. This first part has been a close look at the beautiful treasures that emerge from the fights and struggles of life. I hope you are discovering some of these hidden treasures in your life as you read. But I'm also so excited about this next section because I like an action plan. When anxiety creeps in and I start to forget about joy and endurance, or when my perspective starts to shake, I want someone to tell me what I can *do*. These next chapters are close to my heart because they have been my strategy and sustenance through this battle. I believe they'll also help you develop, with the help of the Holy Spirit, a specific strategy for growing stronger in the fight that you face.

WORTH PONDERING

1. In general, how comfortable are you with the idea of joy and sorrow sharing the same space?
2. List some ways your battle has caused a deeper level of compassion.
3. Read any gospel this week and note the times that Jesus expresses any sort of emotion. It's good to see how God-made-man lived in an emotional world in an authentic way.

WORTH DOING

Buy a journal and designate it your Joy Journal. Every day, record a few things that give you joy. Include the big things like life and breath and security, but also include the little ones like good coffee and pink nail polish. As your journal begins to fill, you'll find that it's good reading on the hard days.

Part 2

STRATEGIES FOR GROWING STRONGER THROUGH EVERY BATTLE

CHAPTER 8

Fasten Your Heart to His Love

Strategic Security

Battles are bumpy. Each one is different, but all have one thing in common: a certain sense of shaking. This jostling may feel minor, like a speed bump, or it may be teeth-rattling, like an earthquake, but the shaking is always there and it's always uncomfortable. A Really Big Battle makes us feel as if nothing in our lives is secure.

As a pastor, I have the privilege of being with people in the middle of crisis. I meet them at the hospital after a car accident or at Starbucks when they discover that their spouse has been unfaithful . . . the bank is taking their home . . . their teenager is pregnant. I recognize the look of dazed disorientation in each one because I saw it in my bathroom mirror every day for many months.

In those early days, I thought the shaking would kill me. Now I look back on that season of turbulence, and I realize that it was a huge gift. It was not pleasant, but the same diagnosis that threw all my earthly security into upheaval also forced me to find a sturdy eternal seat belt and strap in for the battle. Eighteen months later, I can say with confidence that the only security worth trusting is the love of God. His love has been my one constant in an ever-shifting landscape. Before Steve's diagnosis I knew that God loved me, but I had never relied on His love to hold me. Now, however, I know that God's love *works*. His love keeps me held together when everything else falls apart. His love is the only thing that never lets me go. The intensity of the battle has proven the strength and security of His love for me in ways I had never experienced before.

I can't think of a more important strategy for growing stronger in battle than fastening ourselves to the faithful love of God. However, it's not always easy to do. It's one thing to believe that God is powerful or that He is good, but it's quite another to believe that He sees, knows, and adores us personally. Most women I know struggle on some level with the question, *Does God really love me?* We can push our doubts aside when our life feels secure, but big battles bring this question front and center, forcing us to draw some conclusions about the nature of the love of God. I won't kid you here, this can go either way.

DECISION-MAKING MOMENTS

I met Stella several years ago at a class I was teaching about the historical evidence of the life of Jesus. She sat in rapt attention, taking notes, asking questions, and drinking in details like cold water on a hot day. After the class, she flagged me down and seemed frustrated. "Is there anything more?" she asked. "I liked what you taught, but I have so many more questions and I need to dig deeper into this."

I explained that the class was designed as a brief overview but that I could give her some resources so she could do more study. I loaded her up with books and DVDs and prayed for her as she continued her search for proof of the reality of Jesus. A few days later, I met with her over coffee and was surprised to find that she had read every book, watched every DVD, and completed every bit of research I had recommended. While she told me about the progress of her search, I could still hear the same skepticism tinged with desperation in her voice.

"You didn't find what you were looking for?" I asked.

"I don't think I did," she said, as her eyes filled with tears.

Her face was weary and sad, and that's when I realized what she was really seeking. "You aren't looking for proof that Jesus is real, are you?" I asked. "You're looking for proof that He loves you."

Stella swiped at her tears angrily, and her words came out like they were being pried loose from a secret hiding place. "My doubts are not about Him. My doubts are about how someone like Him could love someone like me."

I gave her my best two-minute sermon on how we can know for sure that God loves us. I included Scripture and story and all the truth I know for convincing the broken that they are deeply esteemed and unconditionally loved, but I could tell it wasn't landing. There had once been a time, Stella admitted, when she had known the rich, full love of God. She had loved Him as a child and remembers feeling like the object of His affection. But battle after battle and mistake after mistake had layered up to create a wall of self-hatred as high and strong as any I have ever seen. Stella had painted herself into an untenable position, wanting so much to be loved by God but suspicious of anyone who was stupid enough to risk loving someone like her.

Friend, you can emerge from this battle so scarred and disfigured that you're certain no one could or will ever love you, or you can come out more brilliantly awake and in love with His love. If you let Him, God will show up in every single moment of your fight, and you'll discover the thrill of being chosen and cherished in ways you have never experienced before. But the choice is up to you.

If you are facing the loss of the one thing you believe you cannot live without, you are in the perfect place to discover the true dimensions of God's love for you. Let me ask you a key question: In the depths of your soul where your secret dreams and fears live, do you believe you are unconditionally loved by the Creator of the universe? Do you believe that He sees you and loves you on your best days and on your very worst?

If you can't answer the question with a resounding yes, then it's time to address this issue, once and for all. Now is the time to sink your roots deeply into the soil of His love. There are a few ways to do this, and they are simple but not necessarily easy.

Stop Disqualifying Yourself

Stella had a difficult time accepting God's love for her because somewhere along the line, she began to believe the lie that God loves us because we're good or because we've in some way earned it. Are you familiar with this lie? Big battles will often reveal our biggest inadequacies, but please know that these revelations are not meant to disqualify us from the love of God but to drive us more deeply toward our need for it.

Recently, on a difficult morning, I struggled to focus on the pages of my Bible. My mind wandered in a million other directions, and even though I was desperate for hope from His Word, I ended up spending two hours on the Internet. I shopped. I e-mailed a friend. I watched silly cat videos. I accomplished nothing of value, and in the end I felt emptier than ever. I closed my Bible to get ready for work, and I felt a wave of condemnation so dark and heavy that I leaned against the kitchen counter and squeezed my eyes tight against the feelings that threatened to push me over. Here I was, in the middle of my fiercest battle, when I should be gaining strength from God's Word or praying for my family, and just like the disciples in the garden with Jesus, I couldn't stay in the game. I felt small and hopelessly unfit for His love. Finally, I breathed out a thin prayer: *I am so unworthy of grace.* All I can tell you is that I felt a smile from Him. Not a smirky smile, but a gentle Dad smile. The words that fell into my spirit were, "Were you worthy of it yesterday?"

This time, the smile was mine. No. I didn't earn His grace yesterday. Or the day before that. Or ever. Grace is free. Love is undeserved. And while I know God loves us on the days when we try hard to get it right, I think He's also quite fond of us on the days when we know we'll never get it right.

God didn't love Stella any more before her battles than He does now. Stella loved Stella more before the battle, and she is unable to separate the way she sees herself from the way God sees her. Please know this: God's love is unchanging; His acceptance is complete.

I'm not making this up to make you feel better; the Bible gives us plenty of evidence. In John 13 we find just a small piece of the big story of Jesus' love for His disciples: "And as He had loved those who were His own in the world, He loved them to the last and to the highest degree" (verse 1, AMP). Isn't that beautiful? Verse 3 tells us that Jesus understood that He was about to die on the cross and that this would be His last time to demonstrate His love for His twelve friends before His death (which was the ultimate demonstration). He did so by tying a towel around His waist and washing their feet.

Mary's perfect son, deity clothed in humanity, stooped to the floor and did the work of a slave. The One who would soon wash away every trace of the stain of sin now knelt to wash the dirt of Jerusalem's streets from fishermen's feet. This is a perfect and powerful display of the depth of the love of Jesus for His friends. It's worth noting that Jesus knew that Judas was going to betray Him soon for silver (see verse 2), yet He still washed his feet. Jesus also washed the feet of John, who loved Him. And He washed the feet of Peter, who would deny Him repeatedly. I'm so thankful for these examples because they show us that Jesus' love for us has *nothing* to do with who we are and *everything* to do with who He is.

Knowing all of our failings and fractures—past, present, and future—Jesus still insists on demonstrating His love for us. He still stoops to meet our deepest, dirtiest need. He doesn't do it because we are perfect, but because He is perfect. He is not nearly as enamored with our attempts at awesomeness as we are. He is more drawn to our need for Him and our desire to love and be loved.

Though we dole out our love conditionally, Jesus does not. He welcomes the broken before they're fixed. He opens His arms to children who haven't learned how to be quiet in church (see Matthew 19:14). He forgave an adulterous woman before she even had a chance to promise that she'd never, ever be unfaithful again (see John 8:3-11). And my favorite example is found in Luke 23. As Jesus fought the greatest battle in all of history and hung in the balance between life and death, He was confronted by the two dirty, rotten scoundrels who occupied crosses on either side of Him. One hurled insults and hatred. The other is a man I cannot wait to meet. I'm fascinated by this criminal who experienced a supernatural revelation while enduring the cruelest of all methods of Roman execution. The thief must have known he had wasted his life and squandered his chances to become anything that might make his mother proud. Now his future was numbered in hours rather than days, and even if he wanted redemption, how could he ever find it while dying on a cross? Can you picture the moment that this man caught his first glimpse of Grace, hanging on the cross next door?

He used his strength to shush the other thief, saying,

> "Do you not fear God, since you are under the same sentence of condemnation? And we indeed justly, for we are receiving the due reward of our deeds; but this man has done nothing wrong." And he said, "Jesus, remember me when you come into your kingdom." (verses 40-42)

Remember me. That's an audacious, outrageous request. This bold and brassy criminal didn't try to fancy anything up; he just said it, real and raw: "I've done nothing right and You've done nothing wrong, and yet I'm asking You to love me." As crazy as his request might seem, Jesus' answer is equally mind-boggling: "Truly, I say to you, today you will be with me in Paradise" (verse 43).

What? Did I miss the part where the thief apologized for screwing up? When was he going to earn his stripes and prove his worth and gain this grace? And at what point did he sift through all the evidence to make certain that Jesus was who He claimed to be?

Jesus' response makes the reality of God's love suddenly and supernaturally clear. He promised the thief a place in heaven, the same heaven occupied by Moses and Abraham and David. Without praying a single prayer or attending one church service, without a tithe check or even one day of discipleship training, the thief was ushered in through the gates of eternity by the unwavering love of Jesus.

Here's what these stories mean for you: Who you are and what you've done do not disqualify you from His love. Others may have disqualified you. You may have disqualified yourself. But God has not and He will not. I believe it's an affront to His character when we question His ability or willingness to love us. I could come to your house every morning and tell you this. I could send you texts and e-mails and Scriptures, but none of that will matter until you choose to believe it. Don't feel it? Then just believe it until you do feel it. He loves you. *Choose to believe it.*

Change Your Gauges

Sometimes we determine the measure of God's love by using the circumstances in our lives as our gauge. If we have enjoyed a steady stream of friendships, good health, and happy successes, it's easy to wrap all these good things up in one pretty box, tied with the bow of salvation, and view the package as proof that God loves us. But what happens when one of those items falls out of the box?

Before our Really Big Battle, I had some happy things in my crate of blessings: a great spouse, a safe home, lovely children, and two strong legs. These gifts brought great joy to my life, but they also secretly became the thing that I looked to as evidence of God's love. Without even realizing it, I had confused a lack of suffering in my life with God's unconditional love for me.

The battle with this evil disease immediately did away with the easy proof of God's love that I had relied on for so long. Physical health, finances, family relationships, our dreams for the future . . . ALS rattled so many of the things we felt showed the "favor of God."

Ultimately, this disease pushed us to figure out what it means that God loves us. How do we measure His love when "two strong legs" are no longer an item on Steve's list of blessings? How do we know without question that He absolutely and eternally adores the Family Stern when everything is being shaken? The answer has come for us as we have begun to realize that God demonstrates His love to us with things that will always be ours to keep, not with the temporary joys of living in a temporary world. When I need a reminder of this, I think about some kids I love in Africa, and it resets all the gauges.

On a five-acre plot of land, just outside the hustle and bustle of Nairobi, Kenya, sits an orphanage called Kings Kids Village (http://kingskidsvillage.org). The grounds are lush and tropical, and from a distance it could almost be mistaken for a resort, but a closer inspection shows buildings that are deeply marked by age and weather and wear because money at KKV is invested in heart improvements before home improvements. At the center stands one sturdy building, which is the home to forty-two children, each with a backstory that would be horrifying in our country but is quite ordinary in Kenya. Each one is alone in the world, except for the orphanage staff and the God who loves them. Some of them are afflicted with AIDS; all have been affected by it.

When I visited KKV, I was overwhelmed by the beauty of the kids and their nearly constant smiles. They are taught early on that God loves them, and they believe it. These deeply wounded children who have suffered so much, so young, still bubble over with energy and strength and *life*. KKV struggles month to month just to provide the basics: food, medicine, and an education. The kids there don't have iPhones or iPads or sports equipment or designer jeans. At KKV, those things are not just luxuries, they're impossibilities, and so the staff focuses on giving the kids the one thing that can never be taken from them: an innate, unshakeable awareness of the love of God. These little warriors have faced devastating battles, and yet when you're with them it's almost

100 | *Beautiful Battlefields*

impossible to feel sorry for them. They are rich in the kind of love that is not dependent on what they have or what they lack. It's beautiful and I want to be like them, but sometimes I suspect that the comforts of my country make it more difficult.

In a keep-up-with-the-Joneses society like the United States, it can be hard to kill the tendency for comparison when attempting to measure the love of God. It's easy to question His goodness to us when it seems that He's given all the happy marriages and fat bank accounts and huge successes to other people. This line of thinking is insidious and can creep into our gauges before we even realize it. It crept into mine on the day that a friend who had been worried about his health discovered it was just a minor issue and easily treatable. He rejoiced on Facebook and expressed his gratitude for the great love of God, which had kept him from a truly terrible diagnosis. I really did rejoice with him, but it made me wonder, *What about Steve? Has God still shown him love even though he didn't escape bad news on diagnosis day?*

I felt the sneaky strategy of Satan, tempting me to question whether God's love for us was as good and big as His love for our friend. I had to yank that idea out by the roots (those seed thoughts can turn into big, ugly weeds before we know it). God has shown Himself true and faithful to us time and time again. We can't question His love for us because we're in a battle. Rather, we rejoice in His love that walks us *through* the battle. His love shows up when we think we can't keep going. He comes to our hurting and He pours out His compassion. Sometimes it's through His Word, sometimes it's through the voice of a friend, and sometimes it's just a supernatural infusion of joy when there's no earthly reason we should feel it. But we can say that we know His love better now than we did before because of this battle. That's miraculous, and I believe it's possible for everyone in any kind of fight.

If circumstances are a bad way to measure His love, then how *do* we gain the assurance we long for? Let's turn to the apostle John for the answer. He was so sure of God's love that in his gospel he chose to call himself the disciple "whom Jesus loved" (John 13:23; 20:2; 21:7,20; see 19:26). This is not arrogance; it's confidence. John's entire identity was wrapped up in knowing the love of God. It's a good thing he wasn't measuring it by his circumstances, because his life was filled with suffering, including the crucifixion of his dearest friend, intense persecution for his beliefs, and the deaths of his fellow disciples as martyrs. If anyone had the right to question God's goodness, it was John. How did he manage to remain steadfast and certain that God loved him? He explained it himself in one brilliant sentence that provides all the evidence we'll ever need: "By this we know love, that he laid down his life for us" (1 John 3:16).

It's simple. All of God's love is tied up in that one verse. Jesus poured out His life so that we could know with certainty that we are loved. He will give blessings along the way, and He's never mad when we ask for them. There will be good days and big wins and happy moments, and those are wonderful gifts. But we have to keep the main thing the main thing: The cross proved His love for each one of us, once and for all. From that place, His love flowed out for you and me and John and the thief and everyone who would ever come to believe that He doesn't just give love; He *is* love.

Into each life, fights will fall. As we fasten ourselves to the strong love of God, we will be able to face the battles with confidence, and we will grow strong and beautiful. His love is the wonder of our world, and it holds us together in good times and bad. Believe it; He's crazy about you.

WORTH PONDERING

1. Choose five words to describe the feeling of being perfectly and completely loved.
2. In what ways does the love of God fit the definitions of the words you chose?
3. What is your greatest doubt, fear, or question concerning the love of God?

WORTH DOING

Imagine that you have received a love letter from God. What five words do you think He would use to describe you (because He is good, we know that His words would also be very good). Go ahead and write those words on a piece of paper and put the list somewhere you will see it every day. Fasten your heart to those words when times get tough. It's so good to be reminded that we are loved.

CHAPTER 9

Consult the Captain

Strategic Obedience

When I was in youth ministry, I frequently met with parents who were locked in difficult battles with their teenagers. These moms and dads would often ask formula-based questions, such as "Is it okay to take away privileges because of the way my daughter is behaving?" They were looking for solutions from someone who had walked the road ahead of them. I would have loved to give a set of easy answers that made them feel safe and me smart. However, my response was usually a gentler version of "Is it okay? Sure. Is it *best* in this specific situation with this specific girl? I don't know. This is a God-sized battle, so you need a God-shaped strategy." And then we would pray and ask Him for something divinely designed for the fight in front of them.

When it comes to battle strategy, God is not predictable.

When Gideon was preparing his soldiers to fight the Midianites, God directed him to trim down the ranks by disqualifying thousands of badly needed soldiers because of the way they drank water. Gideon did as God directed and was left with three hundred soldiers, who went on to rout the enemy army (see Judges 7).

Another time, God told Joshua to have the Israelite army walk around a city once each day for six days. On the seventh day they were to march six times in silence and on the seventh time shout (see Joshua 6). I've heard preachers speculate about why this strategy of city circling was so effective, but God chose to use that trick only one time in the Bible. Sometimes I wonder if any other army tried this approach, keeping their fingers crossed that if it worked once it might work again. Imagine how silly the soldiers must have felt when the walls didn't come a-tumblin' down.

In yet another battle, the people of Judah were surrounded by not one, not two, but *three* enemies, and King Jehoshaphat was desperate for divine intervention. He gathered the people together to fast, pray, and ask God for help. Their answer came through the prophet Benaiah, who delivered one of the most encouraging messages ever: "The Lord says this to you: Be not afraid or dismayed at this great multitude; for the battle is not yours, but God's" (2 Chronicles 20:15, AMP).

As Jehoshaphat humbled himself before the Lord, he received a counterintuitive battle strategy and sent worship leaders ahead of the troops instead of warriors. The worshippers began to sing, and the Lord caused the enemy to turn on one another. By the time Jehoshaphat's army arrived on the battlefield, they found only corpses and more spoil than they could cart away.

Three big battles. Three different strategies. I've tried to imagine what it might look like if Steve and I used one of these methods of warfare in our own battle. Making everyone demonstrate their drinking technique before allowing them to fight for us in prayer would be ridiculous. Marching our kids around Bend seems a little extreme. Sending our worship pastors out in front of us as we go to Starbucks? Impractical and annoying to people who just want to enjoy a quiet cup of coffee. It's not that these strategies were silly, but God gave them to those leaders for the fights they were facing, and they probably won't work well for me.

PRAY, LISTEN, OBEY

A deeper look at these stories reveals some strong similarities. Each leader was in a situation with dire consequences. Each knew that a man-devised strategy would not work, and each intently sought God for instruction. Each listened closely, obeyed completely, and experienced great success.

Obedience, it turns out, is always an effective battle strategy. And it is the only one. There is no formula, no one-size-fits-all strategy other than this.

In our fight with this disease, Steve and I have had to make a lot of decisions about his care that will have a significant impact on him and on those who love him. At the time of Steve's diagnosis, Josiah was only eleven years old; these decisions will affect him. Also, we have been praying for many years for some of Steve's friends to find hope and eternal life in Jesus; these decisions will affect them. Each of these decisions is a tiny battle, causing us to turn to God and say, "We don't know what to do, but our eyes are on You." So we pray. Sometimes we fast (desperate times call for desperate measures). We read the Word. We write down what we hear. We discuss it with people we trust. And then we obey. So far this strategy is working.

Early into Steve's sickness, we faced a financial decision so complex and mind-boggling that I won't even attempt to describe it here. Suffice it to say, it was a brain bender and there were no easy answers. We consulted people way smarter than us, and they were all just as flummoxed as we were. So, lacking specific biblical instruction on social security and early retirement issues, we followed the steps of pray-listen-obey. After praying, we both felt as if we heard a still, small voice giving us a daring decision. With a little trepidation, we made the decision, following what we hoped was the leading of the Holy Spirit. Within a few short weeks, God provided a miracle that made the decision make all kinds of sense. We rejoiced in His goodness and in the fact that He is not just the God of Gideon and Joshua and Jehoshaphat but is also the God of Steve and Bo and (insert your name here). He is willing to lead us every step of the way as we listen and obey.

Though this pray-listen-obey strategy is working beautifully in my life, I still find myself on some of the difficult days grasping wildly for a standardized set of instructions. Do you ever feel that way? Have you ever wished you could just buy a foolproof plan that already worked effectively in someone else's battle? As much as we may wish for it, it wouldn't be best for us. Let's explore some reasons that simple obedience, rather than a formulaic set of instructions, is best.

It strengthens our dependence on God.

Formulas are handy because they're prepackaged. Someone else already sought God and heard Him and obeyed with success. Formulas look like a quick trip to an easy win. The principle of obedience feels a lot less secure. It requires that we invest time in a relationship with an invisible God. It demands that we believe we have heard Him and know what He is asking us to do, and that takes practice. It means that we invest our own blood, sweat, and tears into the process of praying, listening, and obeying, and then wait in faith to see the results. It's not easy, but it's oh, so good. In this way, the battlefield keeps us dependent on God and drawn tightly into relationship with Him. This is a not a punishment; it's a gift.

We gain access to supernatural resources and eternal results.

As we seek Him for help, we find that His wisdom is infinite and His power is limitless. Because God sees so much more than we can see, our obedience to His instruction will produce more beautiful and more eternal results than we could ever imagine.

Case in point. In 1967, ethnic tensions in Nigeria spilled over into a vicious and bloody battle known as the Biafran War. It lasted less than three years but left one million people dead from fighting and famine. As coups and countercoups launched Nigeria into the most ferocious fighting her people had ever seen, all foreigners were evacuated from the country. Missionaries and business people were given a chance to get out and were told that no protection would be offered them if they chose to remain. Most of them fled the country immediately for safe havens.

One family, however, did not. They were missionaries in the village of Abraka, which was situated directly in the path of the fighting. This family wasn't crazy, nor did they have a death wish. They didn't even stay because they wanted to. They stayed because they knew with absolute certainty that God had told them to. Here's a piece of the story, the way the wife remembers it, and I think it reads like a battle scene from the Bible:

> When we were invaded by the Biafrans . . . we—and another family with us—didn't know what to do—to leave, as the BBC News suggested for all non-residents, and if so, how were we to go, since there were soldiers in and around our whole area. The first thing we knew that we should do was to ask God about it, so we adults decided we would meet every morning in prayer while the children were doing their school, which we did. Each morning, as we went back to our homes, the kids would ask, "Did God tell you anything?" We would have to answer, "Not yet." In the

afternoon, my husband and another missionary would drive to town to see if there was a ship in the harbor in case the Lord told us to leave. On the third morning, as we were worshipping, the presence of the Lord came among us in a powerful way, and someone (none of us could remember who gave it) spoke clearly, "Stand still and see the salvation of the Lord in your midst." Well, that's all we needed to hear. That very afternoon Paul and the other missionary went to the town of Warri, where a large oil company was based, as they had discovered oil in that area. Long story short, they had sent over 90 American workers home, and told us that we could come and get anything we needed out of their warehouse. Everything we needed during the 6 weeks we were cut off from the rest of the world was there in that huge warehouse. We kept track of everything, and when the war was settled, we went to pay them and the boss said, "Funny, I don't remember you getting anything from us."[1]

Can you imagine the trust that is required to stay in harm's way when everything in you screams to move your four children to safety? I can't imagine. This family stayed and did not just survive. The stories they share of God's supernatural and extravagant protection through that war have been faith-building for everyone who has heard them. Many people, including me, would say that exposing your kids to that level of trauma would surely do long-term, irreversible damage. Not so in this case. The parents' determination to obey God and see Him do the things they could not has set the baseline for the faith of those four children. All of them are successful, loving adults, serving God in all corners of the world, from India to Nebraska to an orphanage in Africa to . . . Bend, Oregon. I am convinced that the experience of facing a civil war when he was a little towheaded boy in Africa has enabled my husband to live his life with a level of faith that many people haven't encountered yet. Steve knows that the same God who kept his family safe when they chose to stay in the heat of the fight will certainly save *our* family when we face a towering enemy.

Now, I know Paul and Eleanor Stern would never suggest that staying in the path of danger is a formula for blessing. No. It's often a formula for a trip to the hospital. Besides, many missionaries left the country at that time and were also saved and blessed. No, my in-laws' determination to stay didn't save them; their commitment to pray, listen, and obey saved them. This is a foolproof battle strategy because it absolutely will work for anyone, anywhere, in any war.

Why did God ask the Sterns to stick it out? For a lot of reasons, I'm sure, but one that circles through the back corners of my mind makes me want to cry. What if God required that level of obedience from that particular mom and dad because He alone knew that one day their boy would face a giant so big that he would want to run for his life? What if God led them to a battle, and kept them in that battle even when they could have fled, so that forty years later my husband could have the most difficult talk of his life with his children and confidently say to them, "This fight is really big, yes, but I know—I *know*—that God is with us."

ASK FOR THE NEXT STEP

Let's visit your battlefield for a moment. What are you facing today that looks impossible? Are there decisions looming like giants? If you don't know which way to go or what to do next, pray. Ask. Find a quiet minute to sit with His Word and let Him speak. Take a look at your fight with His Word by your side and don't be afraid to ask for the next step.

Maybe you've clearly heard the next step and you know what He's asking you to do, but it seems too difficult or too costly. I've been there, friend, and I know it's hard. But I want to cheer you on today and say, Don't wait to obey. God knows what He's doing, and He sees so much more than you can see. Your obedience will build something beautiful for you and maybe even for generations that come after you. Wouldn't that just be something?

If the obedience in front of you requires more strength than you feel you have, you might need a good army. Read on for strategic ways to recruit help and support for the fight that you face.

WORTH PONDERING

1. Imagine you are Joshua and you've been instructed to march around Jericho. List all the roadblocks to your obedience.
2. Is there anything you feel God is asking you to do right now in your battle? What are the roadblocks for you?
3. What part do you think courage plays in obedience?

WORTH DOING

It would be impossible to list all the rewards that will come from your obedience, so instead, dream a little about how your obedience might help create a beautiful win on your battlefield.

CHAPTER 10

Get a Good Army

Strategic Companionship

In October of 2010, I made a list, the most important list I have ever made: a valuable lineup of names. That scrap of paper has become much more than a handy reference tool. It's a lifeline.

For nearly two weeks after I realized that Steve was dealing with something far bigger than either of us had ever dreamed, I struggled to keep myself upright. I couldn't eat. Couldn't sleep. Couldn't think straight for more than a second or two. You see, up until this point in my life, whenever I faced something scary or difficult, I turned to Steve. He is strong and gentle and perfect in crisis situations. He has always been my primary go-to person when I am in pain or in need of help and support. He is the one who holds me up when I find myself about to speak to a large crowd and am suffocated by the certainty that I have *nothing* to say. He is the one who tells me the noise in the house at night is just a noise in the house at night. He is my dearest friend. My default is to turn to him with my fears and failures.

Enter Goliath. Suddenly (literally in about ten seconds) I found myself up against a bigger, scarier fight than I could have ever imagined, and I really *could not* turn to Steve with the depths of my pain. At this point, ALS was only one possibility on a long list of other less-frightening diagnoses. Steve is a man of great faith and did not want to imagine that anything serious was going on in his body, and I did not want to be the one to shake his faith, though I felt deeply that this situation was dire. Explaining my other reasons wouldn't be interesting or helpful, but trust me when I say that I was bereft and on some days feared the future so much that I felt I would be crushed beneath the weight of the *what ifs*.

My next dearest friends, right after Steve, are my daughters. While they knew ALS was on the radar, we wanted to downplay that possibility until we had a concrete diagnosis. Many of the things that kept me from turning to Steve kept me cautious with my daughters as well. So while everyone was fighting the same battle for the same reasons, in that season I no longer had my support team.

That's when I knew I needed to make a list.

I sat down at my table and began writing names, starting with my mom and sisters. The list went on and on. When I was done, I had nearly thirty names.

Each person on my list was a beautiful treasure, unique and strong in an area I knew I would need. My sisters and mom are absolutely the most faithful, loyal, and unshakable women I know. One friend I named can bring joy to the most difficult situations, and this has made her invaluable to me for thirty years. Another is a fantastic listener. The one thing every woman had in common was a heart to help others in battle. Each had an awareness of the power of God and His purposes, and I knew that not one of them would allow me to sink into the muck of despair without a fight. Oh, how I love these beautiful women of God!

Now, it's one thing to have names of friends in your pocket; it's another thing to use them. I don't like to need people, and I don't like to ask for help. I believe that only a battle this big could have made me do what I did next. After making my list, I sat down and picked out about five people and sent them e-mails. I don't remember what those e-mails said, but I know it was not a whole lot more complicated than this: *Steve is very sick and I am dying inside and I really need you.* I read them over once and then pushed "send." In record time, I had five amazing e-mails back, and I don't remember exactly what they said either. I just know they were beautiful and loving and dear. Each one said something along the lines of, *I'm in. No matter what you're facing and no matter where this is headed, I'm here.*

Within twenty minutes, my list of names had evolved into an army of friends. And they have helped me fight this battle by enveloping me with love and words and meals and jokes and cards and copious amounts of Twinkies. They have cleaned my house and picked up my kids and quietly sent their husbands to do some of the heavy lifting and light-bulb changing that Steve's muscles can't do anymore. Most of them have said, "Any time—day or night—you call me when you need me." A woman can live a long time and not run into even *one* three-in-the-morning friend, and yet I have found myself surrounded with many. I never would have known they were out there without this battle, and even with it, I wouldn't have known if I hadn't asked for their help. Sometimes I think we wait for our army to find us instead of asking God to help us identify those who can help us in the heat of the fight.

Believe me, I know it's hard to ask. We women are so hard-wired to meet everyone's needs that we feel ashamed to admit we are up against something too big, too scary, or too strong to handle on our own. But I'm learning that Jesus shows up when we let other people share the sacred spaces of our pain and joy and sorrow, and our willingness to be authentic gives everyone else permission to be authentic as well.

Here are some ways an army of friends can multiply your strength in the middle of battle.

YOUR ARMY KEEPS YOU HONEST

Before he was a missionary, my grandfather had been a butcher, and one of my favorite memories of his visits to our house was watching the flash of steel-on-steel as he sharpened my mom's knives. The blades whistled as they connected with the edge of the tool, moving so quickly that I thought they might spark into flames. My grandpa explained to me that it wasn't the strength or speed he used that made the sharpening process effective; it was the angle at which he held the knives. He said that working at the wrong angle would be worse than not sharpening the knife at all.

The Bible uses this sharpening process to describe the work of our friends in our lives: "As iron sharpens iron, so one man sharpens another" (Proverbs 27:17, NIV).

In a Really Big Battle, when it seems that everything is spinning or that the floor could drop out from under us at any moment, we need friends who are willing to help us stay true to ourselves and to our commitment to Jesus. They can often see things we can't see because we're stuck inside our circumstances. Our friends are on the outside where the view may be clearer.

At the beginning of our fight, I made some decisions that I shared with my friends, and I asked them to help me stay true to those commitments. For instance, I knew that strangers and acquaintances would have many things to say to us about faith, healing, health, and ALS. I also knew that not all of these things would be helpful or encouraging. Determined to avoid wasting time on anger or frustration, I deputized a small posse of close friends to smack me on the hand if I started resenting people who said the wrong thing when really there is no true *right* thing to say. I thought I was doing well with this until one day while having coffee with a friend, I complained about a clumsy comment that kept coming up in conversations with people who don't know me well. She was sweet and accommodating the first couple of times I mentioned it, but by the sixth or seventh time, she smiled kindly and said, "Okay, Bo, it's time to let that go now. You don't have the energy to invest in this." I am stronger in battle today because of my friend's loving, honest words.

This is the kind of sharpening that takes place in relationship, and I really do believe my grandfather was right: Angle is everything. My friends have earned my trust and love, and they exhort me from an angle of redemption and restoration. I know they want the best for me, so I can handle a little steel-on-steel from them. That's not to say it's always easy to hear, but I value their "sharpening" because I know it will make me more effective in battle.

One day I was making an important ministry decision that would have required a huge commitment of time and energy. I wasn't sure I had the capacity to do it, but I'm not good at saying no, so I said yes. Within a few days, several dear friends came to me to say that they would support me if I went through with the commitment but that they were concerned I was stepping outside decisions I had made to prioritize my family and keep my ministry schedule manageable. They were absolutely right. It wasn't too late to cancel, so I made the call and almost immediately felt a thousand pounds roll off my shoulders. I am so thankful for my army of friends who sometimes fight for me by correcting me. This has saved me so much headache and heartache and has preserved my energy for the battle at hand.

Do you have friends who will help keep you honest? Have you

given them permission to speak into your life when they see something that you cannot? I don't think the sharpening process is comfortable for anyone involved, but it's necessary if we want to grow stronger and more skilled in battle.

YOUR ARMY HELPS YOU SEE THE BIG PICTURE

In 2 Kings 6, an angry Syrian army wanted to take Elisha back to their king, so they snuck in at night and surrounded the city where the prophet was staying. When Elisha's servant saw the armies encircling them, he panicked and cried out to his master, who said, "Do not be afraid, for those who are with us are more than those who are with them" (verse 16). It's great how Elisha spoke in faith there, but take a look at what he said next. "Then Elisha prayed and said, 'O LORD, please open his eyes that he may see.' So the LORD opened the eyes of the young man, and he saw, and behold, the mountain was full of horses and chariots of fire all around Elisha" (verse 17).

Oh, I love this! Elisha didn't want the young man to just take his word for it and get on with the battle. He wanted him to actually *see* the proof of the power of God in the same way that Elisha himself was seeing it. He wanted to help open eyes that were fixed on the natural so that they could see into the supernatural and find courage there. I am blessed to have friends exactly like Elisha. They show me the armies, both human and superhuman, that are with us on the days when it's hard for me to see them.

One such fighter in our army is our son-in-law, Corey. He is strong and honest and perfectly suited for our oldest daughter. When we saw the freight train of this diagnosis coming down the tracks, I worried that Corey would feel overwhelmed by the level of need into which our family was moving. He hadn't signed up to take care of a whole family; he had signed up only for Whitney.

One night, shortly after Steve's diagnosis, we gathered our family together for a time of worship, prayer, and planning for the future. At one point, I shared my feelings of fear with Corey. "I know this isn't what you expected when you married Whit. I'm not going to apologize for it, because I think God called you to this, but I hope that you don't feel overwhelmed."

Corey shook his head and said, "No, I'm not overwhelmed. I've been thinking about Ephesians 2 and how it says that 'we are his workmanship, created in Christ Jesus for good works, which God prepared beforehand, that we should walk in them' (verse 10). I was made for this. I was made to walk this road with this family."

I looked around at my family and suddenly I could see it too: the bigger picture. Each of my kids was uniquely created for the life that God knew they would face. Each are compassionate and strong. They were not panicking or running in fear. They were ready. I had been looking at them as helpless victims of an unstoppable giant, but Corey reminded me that they have been placed in this family on purpose because they are each an essential part of this army. He helped pry my vision away from the problem and toward the provision.

The battle looks fierce, yes, but the bigger picture is this: Our dear Father, knowing who we are and possessing all the power necessary to keep this lightning bolt from striking, chose instead to catch it in His bottle and use it to make us complete in Him. When I keep my eyes focused on this big truth, I feel strong for the fight, but sometimes my arms get heavy and my vision droops low. I need friends like Corey who remind me that God is at work in us through this trial and that His plans will prevail.

Some friends excel at giving comfort in hard times, and we all need those kinds of people in our lives. But we also need some brave Elishas who help us see that God is working to bring us through our suffering. I don't know where I'd be without these faithful fighters.

YOUR ARMY SHARES YOUR BURDEN AND LIGHTENS YOUR LOAD

Tucked away between Judges and 1 Samuel is a sparkling little gem of a story that exemplifies faithful friendship. Ruth 1 tells the tale of the family of Elimelech and Naomi, who fled a famine in Bethlehem and looked for sustenance in enemy territory. They set up camp in Moab and found more than food; they also found wives for their sons. When disaster struck and all the men of the family died, Naomi was left with no other option than to return to her homeland. The story says that she left "full" but was now "empty" (verse 21). This was the opposite of a victorious homecoming.

Naomi implored her daughters-in-law to return to their own mothers, to find new husbands, and to enjoy "home and rest" (verse 9, AMP). She had no further claim on their companionship and nothing to offer them except bitter reminders of the life they used to share with the men they loved. One went back, but one would not. Ruth refused to return to the security of Moab and instead became a partner in Naomi's pain. She didn't just sympathize with her mother-in-law's battle; she joined her on the battlefield. As they returned to Naomi's homeland, heads down and hope deferred, they were the talk of the town. Tongues tend to cluck around a good tragedy, don't they?

Ruth rose to the challenge and became the sole breadwinner for the two of them. It couldn't have been an easy assignment. Naomi's new identity was "bitter" (verse 20, AMP). But Ruth was committed to the fight, and she lifted Naomi's load. She fed her, comforted her, and created a new life for herself and her mother-in-law. It's just beautiful, isn't it?

While Ruth's actions were extraordinary, I have found that the spirit of Ruth lives in so many of the people who have lent their strength to our fight. Two friends have taken my son in as their own whenever he needs a place to escape for a while. One friend shows up every week throughout the summer to mow our lawn. My neighbor Corrine lives alone but "accidentally" makes enough dinner for four extra people on a regular basis. On one difficult morning, I headed out the door on the way to work and found that all our flower beds and planters had been filled with bright spring flowers by a mystery friend.

These acts of service, and a hundred more like them, have made all the difference in the fight I'm facing. They have brought life and hope and joy in a season when those things can be hard to find. And whenever they occur, I think of Naomi, and I realize that I have many Ruths in my army who are helping me create a new life inside of difficult circumstances.

Battles all look a little different. Some are physical, some financial, others emotional or spiritual. All are exhausting. It takes energy and strength to face a big fight. Some things only I can do, like be a wife to Steve and a mom to my kids, but there are plenty of things other people can do. Learning to not just allow but *invite* others to share a part of the load is making it so much more manageable to carry.

One caution: Don't assume your friends automatically know what your needs are. Many would love to help but don't know how and are fearful to impose. I've been blessed to have people just show up randomly to help me, but I've also had to learn to pick up the phone and ask for the help I need when I feel I'm in over my head. It's humbling, yes, but humility is not bad, and help with the laundry is very, very good.

If the day looks difficult and your load is heavy, ask God to show you a Ruth or two, and then be willing to invite her in to your battle. You'll be amazed at how good it feels to borrow a little strength from friends. If you cannot think of one friend you can rely on right now, put that need on the top of your prayer list. With confidence I can tell you God desires that we not walk or fight or suffer alone, and He is the giver of good gifts. Ask Him for a faithful friend and believe He will provide one at just the right time.

As you consider the people in your life, here's a truth to hold on to: Not all of them will be able to add strength to your battle. Some aren't ready. Some never will be, so . . .

THIN YOUR RANKS IF NECESSARY

Everyone I know has a Worst-Case Scenario friend. WCS friends are gifted at catching every potential mistake or anything that could possibly go wrong in the near, distant, unforeseen, or never-to-be-seen future. They see pitfalls rather than possibilities.

The psalmist David must have had some WCS friends too. Look at this verse:

> I've already run for dear life
>> straight to the arms of GOD.
> So why would I run away now
>> when you say,
>
> "Run to the mountains; the evil
>> bows are bent, the wicked arrows
>
> Aimed to shoot under cover of darkness
>> at every heart open to God.
> The bottom's dropped out of the country;
>> good people don't have a chance"? (Psalm 11:1-3, MSG)

You can almost hear the panic in the voices that are telling him to run. "Take cover! Find something safer than an invisible God!" Many variations on this theme exist. Sometimes it's the posse of girlfriends who surround the woman in the middle of a nasty divorce and push her toward bitterness. Sometimes it's the ones who label a friend's medical diagnosis the judgment of God. Sometimes it's a friend who feasts on whatever gossip a crisis creates. Though the mode of operation varies, the one thing that consistently reveals a discouraging friend is the way you feel after a conversation. If you feel frustrated, confused, guilty, sad, angry, or just cloudy in general, it may be that your friend is adding gas to the fire instead of water.

Remember that healthy friendships will make you feel loved, upheld, encouraged, and safe. They don't leave you feeling suffocated or irrationally dependent on that person. Good comrades-in-arms will always help you run to the right refuge. They'll help you see the possibilities inside the big mess of impossibilities. And they will lend you their faith and vision to see beyond the moment when yours have grown small and dim.

In difficult seasons, when we already feel outsized by our enemy, it can be tempting to look for safety in numbers and gather anyone who is willing into our army. Big fights, however, require the faith and obedience of Gideon, whom we talked about earlier. Gideon followed God's instruction to cut back his already overmatched troops to just three hundred men. Clearly, God knows that taking the *right* people into battle is a powerful strategy.

Although it's hard to ask others for help, it can be even more difficult to ask a friend to sit a battle out. Sometimes no words are necessary, but a moment may come when you need to have an honest conversation with a friend to explain your strategy for fighting with faith and show her how her words are working against it. If she is unwilling to change, it may be time to stop talking with her about your battle and turn instead to friends who add strength.

A friend who was fighting a fierce battle was forced to make some difficult decisions about the people who belonged in her army. "I was barely surviving," she says, "and the last thing I needed were questions and statements from people that sapped my energy and made me want to give up. I learned I would have to surround myself with people who strengthened me and stay away from people who did nothing but upset me. This decision brought many changes into our lives and caused us to seek out people who were heavily motivated by mercy and grace, which helped us survive and hold on to our faith."[1]

Refusing to live in isolation can make all the difference in battle. Boldly ask God for an Elisha and a Ruth. You can trust Him to give you friends who will help you be honest, keep you focused on the big picture, and lighten your load. He is an army-building God, and He knows what you need before you need it. Now is the perfect time to ask.

WORTH PONDERING

1. Who are the people in your army right now?
2. How do you involve them in your fight? In what ways have you fought for them?
3. Who is your most encouraging friend, and how does that person encourage and support you?
4. Do you have any friends who are not good for you in the midst of a hard day or a hard fight? Who are they, and how does their influence affect your attitude?

WORTH DOING

If your friends were to ask you how they could help you in the battle that you face, do you have a good answer? Write down a few ways your friends could add strength to your fight, even if it's just a specific way that they can be praying for you.

CHAPTER 11

Live the Adventure of Giving

Strategic Generosity

In December of 2010, Dr. Wendell Smith went to be with Jesus after a six-year battle with cancer. Because of the far-reaching impact of his life, thousands of people watched his memorial service via a live stream on the Internet. Wendell was one of our favorite instructors in college, so Steve and I sat on our couch watching and weeping with the multitudes who had been blessed and strengthened by this man's great gift of faith. The service was beautiful in ways I cannot describe.

I went to bed that night and tried to replay that three-hour service in my mind. As I reviewed the tributes from family, friends, and pastors all over the world, it struck me that one of the primary words used to describe the life of that man of God was *generous*. People spoke of the money he had given to missions and ministries and projects and churches. A friend later reminded me of the time Wendell had taken off his jacket and given it to a man in the audience who had admired it. None of Wendell's possessions were out of God's reach; they were all up for grabs to bless the world. A life of extravagant generosity was not just a discipline to him; it fueled his dreams and ordered his priorities. The fruit of generosity had never looked more delicious. Wendell's life made giving look like so much *fun*.

As I lay there, I asked God to help me nourish and produce generosity again in abundance. When the earth begins to cave in, when a relationship crumbles or a diagnosis comes crashing in or a financial earthquake shakes our previously secure foundations, our automatic reaction is to grope wildly for (and grip tightly) anything that remains. In seasons of battle, the fruit of generosity is often the first to wither from the trees.

PRACTICING DAILY GENEROSITY

When Steve's health began crashing in 2010, it felt as though my future was crashing with it, so I found myself looking for anything I could control. I became tightfisted with my time and sparing with my investment in others. One Sunday I was physically unable to write our tithe check. I just couldn't *let go and let God* when it felt as if that money was the only thing standing between me and complete financial collapse. I knew it was ridiculous. Jesus has proven His faithfulness in our finances at least a thousand times in the course of our marriage, but still I was gripped with an irrational panic that prevented me from trusting Him with our money when the chips were down.

After watching Wendell's memorial, I made a solemn commitment to do something generous every day. Now, maybe that sounds like a check-the-box approach to a decision that ought to be Spirit-led, but I know that in order to get good at anything, you have to practice, practice, practice. Isaiah 32 says, "A generous man devises generous things, and by generosity he shall stand" (verse 8, NKJV). Armed with a fresh passion and that verse, I set out each day determined to devise something generous.

Each day God has put something or someone in my path, presenting me with a great chance to give generously. Surprisingly, only about half of those opportunities to be generous have involved money. The rest have been built around things that can be even harder to part with, such as approval, grace, encouragement, and time. I have often been stingy with these important resources, and the Holy Spirit keeps challenging me to give them extravagantly. I'm amazed at how often I don't want to, but these moments of self-discovery are both humbling and freeing.

I remember one emotional and difficult day when the opportunity to be generous came as I was paying the bill in a restaurant that I'm fairly certain had offered us the worst food service in history. I am not generally a reluctant tipper, but I'm telling you, the service was really, really lousy. As I put pen to paper, intending to make a loud statement with my tip, I heard God whisper, "This is your chance to be generous."

"But, God," I protested, "down here where I live, the tip is actually *earned* and it lets the server know how well she's doing."

"But, Bo," He responded, I imagined with a smile, "how would you want *Me* to tip *you* based on how you're doing with generosity?"

A slow learner, I kept arguing. "Well," I reasoned, "I don't think she deserves it."

"Yes," He agreed (finally), "and that's what makes it so generous."

Game, set, match: God.

I wrote down a number on the tip line that astounded even

me, a number larger than any number I had ever written on any such line. It was a tip of epic proportions! And then the funniest thing happened: That silly number smiled up at me and I smiled back. And then I laughed a little bit over the shared knowledge that we — me and my money and the Holy Spirit — were working as a team to *bless* the world instead of as a tool to correct its bad behavior. I felt free and fun. It was lovely. These things may seem small to you, but I believe they are launching the first teetering steps toward a long legacy of generous living.

Steve is also walking out this principle daily. In February he was told that he has a limited number of minutes left in his earthly account, and I wondered how he would choose to spend them. He also has a limited amount of strength to speak, and his therapists warn him often that pushing to the point of fatigue will accelerate the atrophy. I am jealous for his voice; I have always loved it so much, and I want him to be able to tell me he loves me for as long as he possibly can. However, he is an innately generous man, and every day — literally *every* day — you will find him meeting with one friend for coffee, another for lunch, another in the afternoon. By the time I get home from work, he has spent his day encouraging people. He is tired and his voice is tired, but he has determined to live generously with his minutes and muscles.

His friends know that if there is any possible way, he will answer when they call. He has also made the decision to encourage our pastor in whatever way he can with the time he has to do it. He is not going to try to figure out church strategy or methodology; he's simply going to be a source of strength to his spiritual leaders because he wants to live out his days as a generous man. At a time when Steve could have battened down the hatches and tried to protect and preserve his time and words and strength, he is instead scattering them like seeds that will grow into an orchard in the lives of those he leaves behind. I have never been more proud to be his friend, his wife, and the undeserving recipient of his generosity.

GIVING FREELY

Look at what Jesus had to say about living a generous life:

> Judge not, and you will not be judged; condemn not, and you will not be condemned; forgive, and you will be forgiven; give, and it will be given to you. Good measure, pressed down, shaken together, running over, will be put into your lap. For with the measure you use it will be measured back to you. (Luke 6:37-38)

Do you see the encouragement to live generously in every way? Generous with grace and mercy. Generous with forgiveness. Generous with resources. It might sound like giving, giving, giving, but then Jesus added this: It will be given back to you. Jesus was suggesting that however wide we are willing to open our fists and release our resources to a broken world, He will be willing to refill them until blessing spills over our happy hands and into our laps. Here's the picture: You freely sharing your hope and joy and money. Hope, joy, and money rolling your way faster than you can give it away. That's how Jesus works. You just can't outgive Him.

Oh, friend, when life really hurts, it's so tempting to grab all the security you can find and hold it as tightly as you can. It's easy to curl up in the fetal position and block any perceived attempt to take advantage of your dwindling resources. Could I suggest that while that reaction is natural, the opposite response is *supernatural* and therefore produces supernatural results? You can be free, live freely, and give freely, even in the middle of your darkest, fiercest fight. Generosity is a brilliant battle strategy that serves to increase our courage and our undivided faith in the God who will provide.

I want more than anything for God to be able to trust me with resources and to release me to distribute them freely and joyfully to a world hungry for hope. And when I eventually stand before the Giver of every good gift, I want to be able to tell Him that I gave Dr. Wendell Smith a run for his money.

WORTH PONDERING

1. If you could give anything to anyone right now, what would it be?
2. What are two action steps you could take immediately to cultivate a more generous, free life?
3. Dream big for a minute. What might be the results of living with a loose grip on your resources every day for the next one, five, or fifteen years?

WORTH DOING

Give something away today. It could be something material like money or it could be something intangible like approval or encouragement or a smile. Just make sure you are generous.

CHAPTER 12

Run to a Reliable Refuge

Strategic Passion for the Word of God

A baby is supposed to bring life and laughter into a home. That's the rule, right? Julie found that to be true when she gave birth to a healthy baby boy, but everything changed two years later when her daughter Kelsey was born with a rare genetic disorder. From that moment, Julie and everyone who loved Kelsey endured anguish as they watched that beautiful baby experience relentless suffering for the two and a half years that she lived.

I can't imagine anything harder than watching a child live in pain. When Kelsey was ten days old, Julie had to learn to place a long tube through her baby's nose and into her stomach so that she could eat. She would eventually be in charge of administering thirty-six medications per day while trying to comfort a baby who got no relief from the vomiting and diarrhea associated with

131

her condition. At times Julie thought she would suffocate in the stress and heartache. But she moved through each day, finding the strength she needed to go step by step, until finally Kelsey's little body gave up the fight.

As she worked tirelessly to create a secure and loving environment for her sick child, and afterward, when the grief and sorrow of losing her baby set in full force, Julie found a few essential strategies for surviving and growing stronger in battle. One of those strategies was to run to the Word of God for dear life.

Sometimes we make reading and studying the Bible items on the Christian chore chart. Necessary-but-not-enjoyable disciplines to do so that God will bless us. But this view is shortsighted and ignorant. The Bible is so much more than a collection of ancient writings; it is living, active, and vibrant with power for the fights that we face.

While it's easy to tell those in battle to turn to the Word of God for help and answers, it's hard to read and focus on the Bible when Goliath is breathing down your neck. But that is exactly the time we most desperately need the Word.

"I didn't have time to attend Bible studies, read Christian books, or memorize large portions of Scripture," Julie says, "but I found a few Scriptures, and those were what I used to guard my heart and gain strength for battle. I put Scripture cards on my makeup mirror, in my back pocket, in my purse, and on my daughter's bed. God's Word can fight a battle when you are worn out and have no fight left."

Julie wasn't trying to impress anyone or check the boxes in a Bible reading plan. She needed something to hold on to that would sustain her in the heat of the fight. Does that seem like a selfish reason to turn to the Word? I don't think so. I think the Bible was built for battle.

I love Psalm 119. The longest chapter in the Bible, it is fitting that its central theme is the beauty of the Word of God (which the psalmist referred to as "your law" or "your statutes"). Nearly everything we need to discover about the Bible as a battle strategy is woven into this beautiful chapter, including one big reason for running to the Word in the first place: trouble.

> It is good for me that I was afflicted,
> > that I might learn your statutes. (verse 71)

> Before I was afflicted I went astray,
> > but now I keep your word. (verse 67)

> If your law had not been my delight,
> > I would have perished in my affliction. (verse 92)

> Trouble and anguish have found me out,
> > but your commandments are my delight. (verse 143)

Can you see the images here? The psalmist used trouble and anguish and affliction as the flashing arrows that directed him to run to the Word of God. I hate trouble because it makes me feel trapped. I can't fight ALS, so my only option is to run. But to where? Many cheap, easy escape routes exist for women in battle. We can run to the mall or the gym or the Internet. We can run to fantasy or fiction or inappropriate friendships. We can even run to nice-looking refuges, like work or ministry. Now, most of these are not necessarily wrong in themselves, but they are wrong if we choose to run to them instead of to the Word. Few things provide such a reliable refuge and strength for battle. Let's go back to Psalm 119 to discover why.

THE WORD IS UNCHANGING

In a constantly shifting world, where relationships, values, and trends come and go, the Word stands unmoved. Many discredit its value because of the changes in culture since the time it was written, but this, to me, is exactly why it's so wonderful. The Bible doesn't budge when everything else does, which enables us to know truth. Look at what the writer said about the unwavering nature of the Word of God:

> Forever, O LORD, your word
>> is firmly fixed in the heavens. (verse 89)

> Long have I known from your testimonies
>> that you have founded them forever. (verse 152)

> The sum of your word is truth,
>> and every one of your righteous rules endures forever.
>>> (verse 160)

The Word is not a quick fix; it is an eternal refuge in the middle of our temporary battles. It was steady and secure long before our arrival on this spinning orb, and it will remain long after we are gone. From forever to forever, the Word of God is situated for our good.

THE WORD MAKES OUR WAY STRAIGHT AND SAFE

Not only is the truth in the Word unchanging, but it is also meant to guide our decisions and behavior. The Bible helps clear a way through the clutter and confusion, shining a light on the path we should take.

Your word is a lamp to my feet
  and a light to my path. (Psalm 119:105)

Lead me in the path of your commandments,
  for I delight in it. (verse 35)

I shall walk in a wide place,
  for I have sought your precepts. (verse 45)

Great peace have those who love your law;
  nothing can make them stumble. (verse 165)

I hold back my feet from every evil way,
  in order to keep your word. (verse 101)

Julie remembers a time when she didn't know if she would make it. The weight of her circumstances seemed like too much for her small, shaking arms to carry. She cried out to God and immediately felt the whisper of the Holy Spirit say, "Just be Mom to these children for the next hour." She thought about it and returned to the verse she had depended on throughout her battle: "I can do all things through him who strengthens me" (Philippians 4:13). She decided that maybe she could be Mom for another hour. And then came the next hour. And the hour after that. That small eternal sentence from the beautiful Word of God fueled each one of those hours with the strength she needed for the long haul. When she wanted to run another direction, the Bible directed her path and kept her straight and safe.

I remember a day when I was facing a difficult meeting at work; I was passionate and anxious about the issues that would be discussed. Early in the morning, I woke up with arguments and rebuttals racing through my mind, all preparation for the conversation ahead. As I stumbled into my prayer room and opened my Bible, my eyes landed squarely on the words of Psalm 62: "My soul, wait only upon God and silently submit to Him; for my hope and expectation are from Him" (verse 5, AMP). *Silently submit to Him.* I knew without any doubt that those words were the light for my path that day. It was not a day for defending my position or arguing my point; it was a day for trusting God to do the talking. I did, and I have always been thankful I stayed quiet that day. This has been my story countless times: The Word directs my path, my decisions, my life. It is a safe compass, and its direction can be trusted.

THE WORD GIVES LIFE AND HOPE

From the time David was anointed king of Israel (see 1 Samuel 16) until the time he assumed the office of king (see 2 Samuel 2), he endured long years of battle with King Saul and just about everyone else in the vicinity of the throne. Twice he hid in a cave. Once he pretended to be crazy. Twice he turned to his enemy for refuge. In 1 Samuel 30, he and his army of malcontents returned home to find that their wives and children had been kidnapped by the Amalekites. Then his own men wanted to kill him. In that battle David wept until he had no strength left to weep. In spite of his success and favor with God, David was no stranger to heartache, fear, suffering, or desperation. The secret to his survival was that he learned how to strengthen himself in the Lord (see 1 Samuel 30:6) through the Word. Read this verse and imagine David hooking up his weary soul to the Word, like a doctor connects a defibrillator to a dying heart: "For by You I can run through a troop, and by my God I can leap over a wall. As for God, His way is perfect! The word of the Lord is tested and tried; He is a shield to all those who take refuge and put their trust in Him" (Psalm 18:29-30, AMP).

Psalm 119 is bursting with this sort of life-giving hope. As you read these verses, connect your heart to the strength they bring.

> My soul clings to the dust;
>> give me life according to your word! (verse 25)

> My soul melts away for sorrow;
>> strengthen me according to your word! (verse 28)

> This is my comfort in my affliction,
>> that your promise gives me life. (verse 50)

> I am severely afflicted;
>> give me life, O LORD, according to your word! (verse 107)

> Uphold me according to your promise, that I may live,
>> and let me not be put to shame in my hope! (verse 116)

> I rise before dawn and cry for help;
>> I hope in your words. (verse 147)

> Consider how I love your precepts!
>> Give me life according to your steadfast love. (verse 159)

The word *life* here means "to quicken or revive."[1] These verses are CPR for the heart that feels crushed, wounded, and weary. An infusion of the Word will resuscitate your dreams and refresh your strength.

Let's look at a couple of ways we can turn to God's Word for hope and help in battle.

Run to read it.

Many silly notions exist about what constitutes a "real" devotional life. When I was young, my youth pastor insisted that three chapters per day had some sort of magical, mythological power to change a life and make God happy. Every January, thousands set out on a pilgrimage to read through the Bible in one year, only to lose heart when February arrives, bringing Leviticus with it. I'm not criticizing Bible reading plans, but this season in battle has made me realize that they are often guilt-producing rather than life-giving.

I love to read and study the Bible. Other people enjoy jigsaw puzzles or hang gliding. This is not an indication of my spirituality but rather something that's hardwired in me. It's not work for me to spend time in the Bible; it's what I do for fun. However, in the early season of our battle, there were days when I was able to make it through only one psalm or three verses in Philippians before my attention span was shot. Sometimes I would end up crying into the pages of my Bible; other times I stared off into space in some sort of catatonic state.

During that twelve-month period, at no time did I ever manage to read three chapters on any given day. Yet the Word was still exactly the refuge and resource I needed. If I had placed human expectations on how much Bible reading is enough, I would have given up. Even now, as I juggle the increased responsibilities that this season in our life demands, I have to remind myself that it's better to absorb one verse than to run my eyes over the surface of a whole chapter and remain unchanged by it. Run to read the Word, friend, with no guilt or condemnation, but rather with wide-eyed anticipation for the life it will bring.

Meditate, speak, and sing it.

Let's revisit Psalm 119 for some inspiration and instruction:

> I will meditate on your precepts
> and fix my eyes on your ways. (verse 15)

Oh how I love your law!
> It is my meditation all the day. (verse 97)

My eyes are awake before the watches of the night,
> that I may meditate on your promise. (verse 148)

With my lips I declare
> all the rules of your mouth. (verse 13)

My tongue will sing of your word,
> for all your commandments are right. (verse 172)

The word *meditate* means "to ponder, to commune or converse with oneself aloud."[2] When we combine that definition with these verses, we see a clear picture of the way the Word can jump off the page and join the constant conversations in our minds. As we ponder the promises of God, they sink into our spirit and become a refuge on our battlefield.

One of the best ways I've discovered for making the Word come alive—especially when my mind is reeling with other things—is to read it out loud. As I hear the words of the Word, they slice through the tension in my heart and the heaviness in my home. They encourage and strengthen me throughout the day.

Though I read the Word in the morning, it is at night when it becomes my dearest treasure. Have you discovered, like I and so many others have, that it's hard to sleep when you are on the battlefield? At night, anxiety and fear swarm like locusts, creating a chorus of noisy thoughts that steal sleep and peace and compound our trouble. David was no stranger to this situation. In Psalm 63 he made a firm decision, and I am trying to adopt it as my own.

I remember you upon my bed,
> and meditate on you in the watches of the night;

for you have been my help,

and in the shadow of your wings I will sing for joy. (verses 6-7)

Nighttime is the perfect time for reflecting on God's goodness and the truth of His Word. When fear wants to sweep in and steal hope, have a verse at the ready so that you can ponder the goodness of God. Speak to your heart. Preach the Word to your soul. Run to His unchanging goodness and find a secure refuge there.

As you find God faithful in the pages of your Bible, you will find His strategy for your battle. He is the God of Abraham, Isaac, David, and . . . you. Run fast and free, friend. The Word is waiting for you.

WORTH PONDERING

1. Think of a time when something from the Word had an answer you were looking for or comfort you needed.
2. What is the biggest obstacle you face in consistently spending time in the Word?
3. Have you ever tried memorizing verses to have at the ready when times are tough? You could pick one from this chapter as a start.

WORTH DOING

Tonight as you go to sleep, run a verse you know through your mind and think about its meaning, its hope, its truth. Ask the Holy Spirit to let those words work in you through the night.

CHAPTER 13

Escape the Weight of Bitterness

Strategic Forgiveness

*F*rederick Bowe[1] *has died.*

The subject line stopped me in my tracks. I opened the e-mail and read the simple note from a coworker, saying he had received word that Frederick had passed away a week earlier and he did not know of a scheduled memorial service. Deep sadness washed over me and tears unexpectedly welled up and spilled over. Frederick and I had worked together on a volunteer team for two years before he left our church for unknown reasons. Though we had spent a fair amount of time together, we had never managed to move beyond being just acquaintances.

I made a few phone calls to see if anyone knew how he had died or if there might be a service for him. The responses I received were remarkably similar. "No, I don't know anything," they

141

would say sadly and then pause before adding, "He was just so bitter." My thoughts exactly.

I have never worked with anyone who radiated such deep dissatisfaction with life in general and with human beings in particular. I enjoy trying to win over curmudgeonly people. It's a challenge to find ways to sneak in the back door and become their friend when they're not looking, and so I really did try with Fred.

I asked him about his life. *Growl.* I asked him about his work. *Growl.* I asked him about nearly everything except for his politics because I don't have the stomach for those conversations. I tried to be funny. *Growl. Sneer.* The closest I ever came to hitting a soft spot was when I asked him about his motorcycle. It was perhaps the one and only thing he loved. I'm assuming he loved it, because he didn't yell at me for asking him about it. In spite of working to know him and reach to his heart, I don't think it ever happened. It's fine that Fred did not want to be friends with me. It's tragic, however, that it appears he wasn't friends with anyone.

Today I looked everywhere for his obituary. I looked for any evidence that he had lived and died and maybe left a mark somewhere that I didn't know about. Maybe he had secretly given money to a children's hospital or visited veterans or even just loved someone once? I found nothing. That's not to say there *is* nothing, but I wish that, if such evidence exists, I could see it. I would love to run into some proof that his life was more than his bitter words, but so far I've come up empty and sad.

I don't have any idea what caused Frederick to become so angry at the world, but if I had to guess, I would say that it happened on a battlefield somewhere. He, like all of us, found himself in a fight for which he was unprepared or overmatched, and the wounds he sustained there left him encased in a suit of thorns so sharp that no one could ever get in to help heal him.

A DEBILITATING SIDE EFFECT OF BATTLE

If we're not careful, any one of us can die in the tomb of our own self-protection. Psalm 73 paints a brilliant and brutal picture of the way bitterness develops and can eventually destroy us.

While many of the psalms were written by David, this one was written by Asaph, who also wielded a mighty pen, especially here. In this passage, he rolled line by line through his frustrations with his current situation. The bad guys were succeeding. Bullies were winning and bragging about it. The rulebook for who deserves blessing had been flipped upside down, and it was causing Asaph great distress. Have you ever noticed how quickly something that began as a justifiable war on injustice can become an internal battle with bitterness? Look at these words:

When my soul was embittered,
    when I was pricked in heart,
I was brutish and ignorant;
    I was like a beast toward you. (verses 21-22)

I had to read that last line several times when I was studying this passage recently. I read it in many translations. I looked at the original language. I combed through the words over and over because it seemed like such an extreme statement. Do you know what I discovered? It really does mean what it seems to mean. Bitterness turns us into a brute beast. We lose sensitivity to God's voice. We can't hear anything over the sound of our own pain, and we trample people who may be just as wounded. Like a water buffalo at a tea party, we become all brawn and no brain; all power and no poise. At best, bitterness is disruptive and ineffective; at worst, it's lonely and destructive.

In the weariness of battle, when our hearts thirst for justice and perhaps even vengeance, how do we keep from drinking bitterness? Paul offered a solid strategy in Ephesians when he said, "Let all bitterness and wrath and anger and clamor and slander be put away from you, along with all malice. Be kind to one another, tenderhearted, forgiving one another, as God in Christ forgave you" (4:31-32).

Well, that's a lot of big truth right there. Here are some points from that one tiny verse that are having a huge impact in my life.

IDENTIFY IT

Bitterness can be a tricky thing to see in ourselves. Sometimes it's obvious and outward, but often it lives as a root, sunk deeply into the soil of our hearts. Bitterness can germinate a long time underground, but it will eventually shoot sprouts through the surface that others can see.

I've found a few great ways to identify these sneaky seeds:

Ask the Lord.

David said, "Search me, O God, and know my heart! Try me and know my thoughts! And see if there be any grievous way in me, and lead me in the way everlasting!" (Psalm 139:23-24).

We root out bitterness by first opening up our lives to the loving attention of the Holy Spirit. In His kindness, He can reveal the things that are hiding that could grow into something ugly and destructive: unhealed hurt, resentment, rebellion, or frustration.

About five years ago, I moved my devotional times to early mornings, mostly just because it was the only time of my day that no one else wanted. Setting aside that before-the-sun time has enabled me to focus on specific things each morning of the week. Some days I focus on praying for my kids or my church or orphans or our extended family. Some days I focus on studying. But one day is always the same. On Saturdays I focus on me.

That is the morning when I open my Bible, take a deep breath, and pray, *Show me my heart. What's inside that I can't see? Is there any seed waiting to become a root or any root waiting to become a fruit that's not worthy of Your kingdom or the price that You paid to save me?*

I do not exaggerate when I say that God *always* responds to this request. Sometimes it's through a verse that pricks my heart. Other times it's the memory of a conversation I had during the week where my words were unkind or untrue or unfair. Often it's the reminder of an opinion I formed about someone else that was born out of jealousy or pride. God always shows up and shows me what I am unable or unwilling to see on my own.

When I first started this practice, I was nervous (maybe even a little fearful) about the idea of hearing the truth about the stuff inside my heart. I am a people pleaser who does not enjoy criticism. I do not want to be told I'm anything other than awesome. But now, with years of Saturdays under my belt, I remain astounded at the kindness and gentleness of our good Father. He responds to the heart that is willing to hear, and then He loves it into change. I would so much rather learn this stuff from Him in the secret place than from the consequences that occur when my bitter fruit comes out of hiding.

Ask Him. He'll show you and help you find the next steps to freedom. The One who made you can surely heal you.

Ask others.

My friend Sonja is one of the most amazing women of God I have ever known. She enjoyed a successful career as an executive for years before she and her husband, John, devoted their lives to writing and teaching a discipleship curriculum. Now, when other couples their age are enjoying a relaxing retirement, John and Sonja are traveling the world teaching thousands about the power of living like Jesus. They are spiritual heroes to me. Imagine my surprise, then, when Sonja invited me to coffee one day to say, "My life is open to you. If you ever see anything in me that appears unhealthy or out of alignment with God's character, would you please tell me?"

I sputtered and stammered for a moment, trying to imagine how I would ever be able to speak into the life of someone I considered to be so much further down the road than I, but she looked me in the eyes and said sternly, "Bo, I mean it. I want you to tell me if you ever see anything that I can't see. Will you do that?"

As I've watched Sonja's life, I've seen fruit that is born of hard work, discipline, and talent. But I also see a woman who has avoided a lot of the mistakes that so many make in ministry. Her marriage, friendships, and priorities are healthy, and she enjoys exponential influence in the world to which she is called. Sonja has lived plenty of time on battlefields, but she demonstrates the joy of living free of bitterness. This abundant life did not come by hiding her flaws from others, but by opening her life to those she trusts.

I know it's scary to let others in, but a simple conversation over coffee is a brave strategy for identifying bitter hot spots in our lives. Select a friend who knows you and knows God and ask, "I know that I cannot see myself as clearly as I'd like to. Are there any areas in my life where you feel I might be hiding some bitterness? Do my words or actions ever make you feel that I am angry at anyone or at God?"

Now, if you suspect you know what your friend will answer, then you have already begun the process of identifying bitter roots. It's important not to stop there. The next step is to put bitterness away.

PUT IT AWAY

When I first began studying Paul's words in Ephesians 4, the idea of putting away bitterness seemed impossible. How do you do that? Where do you put it? What do you do with the hole that's left where the bitterness used to be?

The answer came in looking more deeply at the words of Paul. The original language for "put away" is the Greek word *airo*, which means "to weigh anchor."[2] Bitterness is an extra weight that connects itself to our lives and slows us down. It keeps us tied to the shore rather than sailing into fresh purpose, new adventure, and authentic relationships.

Many of the things that cause bitter roots and fruit in our lives are legitimately hurtful and hard. You are reading a book based on my battle experiences, but I'm guessing you could also write one of your own. Heartache and injustice create a million kinds of heavy weights, and we must choose either to hold on to them or to release them to the providence of God. I want to get really good at joyfully shouting, "Anchors aweigh!" But how? I know of two powerful tools for cutting the strings to bitterness in our lives.

Forgiveness

Many years ago, I was struggling to let go of a difficult relational break that I had experienced with a dear friend. As much as I tried to get beyond it, I kept replaying conversations and conflicts over and over in my head, trying to figure out what had gone wrong and how it ended up in such a mess. One night I was trying to go to sleep, but I just could not get the situation to stay quiet in my mind, and I finally said to the Lord, *Please, will You take this thing from me? I can't keep doing this anymore.* I fell asleep shortly after and had a most remarkable dream that has influenced my concept of forgiveness and freedom.

In the dream, I was standing at the top of a cliff, and beneath me was a wild, raging river. The water was deep, dark, and turbulent, and at my feet sat a large, old trunk. A voice spoke and said, "Take every instance, every conversation, every conflict, every hurtful word, and every painful thought from that situation and put it in the trunk. I'll wait."

I began to think about it, and as I remembered hurtful events—even something little—I put it in the trunk. It was surprising how long it took to replay all those memories. I hadn't realized how much weight I had been carrying from that one relationship and all its turmoil. When I had filled that trunk with every last possible frustration or offense, I closed the lid and waited.

"You know what to do," spoke the Voice into my dream.

I sighed and looked at the river, and then I looked at the trunk, then back at the river, then back at my pile of pain. "I can't," I cried. "I can't throw it in."

"But you said you wanted to be free."

I *had* said that and I had meant it. I really wanted to be free, but I was afraid to let go. "Why am I so afraid?" I asked.

"You know why."

I always hate answers like that, but it made me think more intently about the situation. Why was I holding on to that dumb trunk? It wasn't filled with anything good, just bad memories. Why would I be reluctant to get rid of it? I stood staring at the turbulent water and imagined throwing my pain into its depths, and then it occurred to me. I said it out loud, tears streaming now. "I do want to let go of the pain, yes. But that trunk also contains all the evidence that I was right." I realized that throwing that box of hurt away would be like a lawyer taking the file that proves his case and tossing it out the window of his car. If I let go of the evidence, how would I explain why it was hard for me to trust people or to get involved in a church or to invest in new relationships? For the first time, I understood why people said they would be able to forgive but never to forget.

I stood at the top of that cliff for a long time in my dream, weighing my options and counting the cost of the commitment I was about to make. At one point, the Voice said, "You know, if you throw it over the edge, you can always put on a wet suit and go get it again. It'll just be harder to get to and you'll have to decide if it's really worth it to have it back again."

Decision made. I heaved the trunk over the side and watched it disappear into the inky black water. At first I felt panic, but then I experienced a peace like I have never known. It was beautiful. I woke up and knew I was free.

Have I ever wanted to dive back in and get that trunk? Once or twice, yes, but each time, I remembered the dream and said, "Nope. It's gone and I don't know how to swim." Letting go of my bitterness was one of the most amazing, supernaturally freeing experiences of my life. When I eliminated my need to be right, I began to see many places where I hadn't been. Letting go of all of that weight enabled me to see my own role in the relationship breakdown.

Forgiveness fills the hole that bitterness leaves behind, and it helps you see yourself more clearly. When we determine that we will forgive *and* love, we open our hearts up to the complete healing of the One who gave His life to forgive us. He's not asking for anything He Himself hasn't already done. Isn't it amazing how He always goes first?

Gratitude

I'd never imagined the depths of rejection that people experience until I met Delia. She is a beautiful woman whose happy face and bouncy feet distinguish her on our church's worship team. No matter what song they sing, Delia cannot keep her tiny body from moving along with the music, and her joy just jumps out from the stage and into the audience. Everyone knows Delia. She stands a little over four feet tall; her hair cascades in beautiful black curls down her shoulders and frames her face, which is always lit up with a smile. Fluent in five languages, she also has a law degree, three beautiful children, and a husband she adores.

Most people don't know that Delia's mother tried to have her aborted late in the pregnancy and the procedure failed. No one can see the emotional scars caused from being abandoned on the steps of a hospital at age five. Also invisible are the deep wounds caused by an ex-husband who is now in prison, paying the price for the many ways he inflicted pain and suffering on Delia and her children. Life for my friend has brought sorrow after sorrow, but still she sings. If you ask her how she has maintained joy on her battlefield, her answer will always be the same: "God has been *so* good to me."

Delia has found that the quickest route from bitterness to beauty is through the door of thanksgiving. She overflows with gratitude for her children, her husband, the fact that God kept her alive the many times she should have died, and even the mother who abandoned her and the men who abused her. She sees clearly that Satan's attempts to silence and sideline her were no match for the sovereignty of God, who has moved her into a life of purpose, provision, and joy. She is a thankful woman, and I want to be just like her.

The number one question I am asked right now centers on the theme of how I am able to stay happy in hardship. The obvious and correct answer is that God is amazingly good and He gives supernatural peace. But I've discovered that the process is a bit of a dance in which He leads and I follow. I'm glad I don't have to lead, but I think that learning to follow has required one really big and important discipline: "Enter his gates with thanksgiving, and his courts with praise! Give thanks to him; bless his name!" (Psalm 100:4).

Psalm 100 is called the Psalm of Thanksgiving, and it's the swiss army knife in my survival kit because I know for sure that gratitude will help me cut the strings to overweight anchors of anger and bitterness. Every time I say "thank You," I sever another tie to the sinking feelings that the battlefield creates.

Thank You for Your hand in our lives.

Thank You for our healthy, wonderful kids.

Thank You for such a great relationship with a great man for twenty-seven years.

Thank You for a country filled with fresh air and clean water.

Thank You for Twinkies.

Thank You for the hope of heaven.

I have much to thank God for. But it's not always easy. Nearly every day I fight the temptation to spend a little time licking my wounds and patting my own head. Some days I end up bobbing around in the waters of bitterness before I get frustrated enough to cut the strings to that anchor and enter His gates with some determined thanksgiving. Refusing to dwell on difficulties requires emotional muscle that has been trained in turning bitterness to beauty. I am still working on it and, I hope, growing in it.

I am blessed to lead an amazing group of college-age interns at our church. Recently I declared a three-day fast leading up to Thanksgiving. The fast would not involve food, I told them, but would instead be a fast from all complaining. We would attempt to live out the words of Paul in 1 Thessalonians 5:18 that tell us to "give thanks in all circumstances." During those days we worked hard to grow the muscle of gratitude. When we were late and the traffic light turned red, we thanked Him that we live in a land where traffic lights keep us safe. When we annoyed each other, we thanked Him that we live in a community of grace. When we failed, we thanked Him for second chances. It was hard. But it was also a fantastic, freeing experiment, and it helped each one of us expose some bitter blind spots.

Developing an automatically thankful life is not easy, but it's definitely worth it, because gratitude throws open doors to His presence. It ushers us out onto a balcony with an eternal view, and from there we can see the days of our lives so much more clearly.

I don't want to be the bearer of bad news, but someday, someone will write to someone else and tell her that you have died. With the death rate standing now at 100 percent, it will happen to all of us. What would you want the summation of your life to be? How would you hope your children speak of you? Your best friend? Your coworkers? Now is the time to cut the strings to bitterness and shout a joyful "Anchors aweigh!" Now is the time to feel the wind in your hair as your boat breaks free into the open water. Get moving, friend! Winning the battle with bitterness offers lifelong rewards of freedom, joy, and beauty.

WORTH PONDERING

1. In what ways do you think bitterness makes us less human and more beastly?
2. Have you ever been on the receiving end of unkindness caused by someone else's bitterness? How did it make you feel?
3. What action step might you take this week to begin to discover or break cycles of bitterness in your life?

WORTH DOING

Pick one day this week to abstain from all bitter words, turning complaints and frustrations into gratitude instead.

CHAPTER 14

Speak Strength

Strategic and Powerful Words

Something strange happened to me when I became a mother. Along with the extra baby weight, I put on twenty pounds of discernment and about three thousand pounds of caution. Suddenly, everything from the doorstop to the miniblind cord was a choking, fire, or toxic hazard. Danger lurked everywhere, and I was on the lookout constantly (no wonder being a mom is so exhausting).

One place I assumed would be a safe haven of intellectual stimulus for our kids was literature. I loved books when I was growing up, and I couldn't wait to read to our daughter, so I started when Whitney was just days old. I remember sitting down with my tiny beauty of a girl and pulling out a book of nursery rhymes. The cover was a bright canvas of smiling moon and glittery stars, with a snugly wrapped baby happily floating in between. It was just how I wanted my girl to feel during story time. I opened the book to the first page, saw that the rhyme was one of my favorites, and began to read out loud:

Rock a bye baby on the tree top . . .

Hmmm. Has that always been the first line? What is that little baby doing up in a tree? That doesn't seem safe at all. Where is her mom? Her dad? Is there a net of some sort? A harness, perhaps? And if there is a harness, are we certain the baby will not choke on it?

When the wind blows the cradle will rock . . .

Oh good. The baby has a cradle in the tree. But does the cradle contain any lead-based paint? The wind seems scary, but I guess as long as it only rocks . . .

When the bough breaks the cradle will fall . . .

Heart palpitations. This is not good! And the not-goodness of it is made creepier by the fact that it rhymes!

And down will come baby, cradle and all.

I am not reading this to my child. We'll go to the next one.

But the next one was no better. The nursery rhymes I had come to know and love *all* involved tragedy or child abuse. Turns out, nursery rhymes were predominantly created at a time when freedom of speech was not a civil right. Hidden messages were built into the sweet-sounding rhythms or set to music so that children and adults alike could repeat them without understanding the deeper meaning. In the end, I decided to find happier stories to read to my kids, because words are powerful.

WORDS OF LIFE AND DEATH

During this battle, God has been working to help me understand the weight of my words. Proverbs 18:21 says that life and death are in the power of our words. *Life and death.* Many times I have referred to Steve's diagnosis as "the fight of our lives." In a season this intense, I want to know exactly what causes life and what brings death. If words are as powerful as this verse suggests, they can play a big role in our strategy for becoming stronger in battle.

Dr. Louann Brizendine, author of *The Female Brain*, believes that women use about twenty thousand words every day.[1] Of course this varies from woman to woman, but this is the average. While some may use this number to suggest that women talk too much, I think it's a beautiful number because it gives us a dozen opportunities every minute to choose life instead of death, hope instead of hurting. Isn't that exciting?

How do we harness this powerful force into something that brings healing, hope, and life? I'm sure there are many good ways, but here are three kinds of words that I am trying to speak: true words, building words, and worship words.

True Words

True confession: I am a fan of Barbie. I loved her when I was little, and then I had three daughters, so our house was overrun with those little dolls and all their stuff. One day I discovered an unattached Barbie arm on the counter and decided to go looking for its owner. Riffling through piles of dolls and clothes and detached limbs, I found Barbies with every sort of handicap and in every possible state of disarray. Bad hair. Bad nails. Missing heads. The only consistency in the appearance of those poor little dolls was that each wore a perfect, happy smile. Maybe it wasn't a great hair day for Barbie, but she was not going to show it. As little girls, many of us learned more from Barbie's frozen-in-place smile than we realize.

A lot of us are good at faking it when we are hurting. A friend told me that when her marriage fell apart, she didn't feel she could tell anyone about her husband's secret addictions because they were both prominent leaders in their church. She suspected that the truth would cost them their position and worried that if he were no longer involved in the church, he would have no reason to keep trying, so she held on to her secret as long as she could. Eventually, the battle got too hot to hide, the walls she had built came tumbling down, and the truth was exposed. Though the truth was costly, it also led to the greatest freedom she has ever known, and she continues to discover what it means to live in truth.

Sue was raped in her home two weeks before her husband returned from deployment. Her husband was a volatile man, and she was so afraid of how he would respond that she locked that dark secret deep inside, telling no one. Can you imagine the torment? Six months later she was five months pregnant and having constant nightmares; her husband knew things were not right and she had to tell him the truth. Even though his response was not good, letting it out enabled Sue to begin to heal. Now, more than fifty years later, she says that one of the most important strategies she has learned about surviving a fierce fight is, "Don't keep secrets. The Enemy destroys us with our own secrets."

I am also a recovering secret-keeper. Though mine were not as dramatic as these, they were still damaging. Raised in the church, I have always felt a certain pressure to be happy and good. No one taught me this directly; I just learned it. I fastened on my Barbie smile, even when my arm was falling off, because I feared that a less-than-perfect life would reflect badly on God or my husband or my children or—gasp!—me. Because I've always had close friends to confide in when I was at my worst, I felt okay about making the rest of the world think there was no "worst." Those looking on from outside my circle of confidence viewed a world where the checks never bounce, the kids never fight, and the bathroom is always clean. I laugh looking back on the paragon of virtue I pretended to be, but never quite was.

Several years before our fight with ALS, my shell began to

crack when I discovered that when I spoke to women, the best teaching moments were not built around my successes, but my failures. Slowly but surely, I realized how much we need transparent examples of the grace of Jesus in the community of faith, and I learned to love the fresh air of authenticity. When we met the giant of Steve's diagnosis, however, the idea of faith-filled honesty moved to a whole new level.

As grief and pain nearly knocked me off my feet, I remember a moment when I cried out to God, "I really want to make You look good, but everything hurts so much." The response of the Holy Spirit was swift and firm: "I can be beautiful all by Myself. You just love Me and I'll do the rest." What a relief! While my intention had been good, I realized that I had taken on a weight that didn't belong to me. Now I know that it's okay to be truthful about the hard days, and it's okay to not have all the answers about why God has allowed this tragedy to touch my family. I refuse to believe that authenticity is the enemy of faith.

David modeled a raw but God-focused life.

> Answer me quickly, O LORD!
>> My spirit fails!
> Hide not your face from me,
>> lest I be like those who go down to the pit.
> Let me hear in the morning of your steadfast love,
>> for in you I trust.
> Make me know the way I should go,
>> for to you I lift up my soul. (Psalm 143:7-8)

David brought his pain to God because he knew God could handle it. Like this one, many psalms record David's cries of sorrow to the Lord. David did not hide his pain from the watching world. He expressed it for God and others to hear, and he found healing through it. Do you know who else did this well? Jesus.

Luke 22 tells the story of Jesus' final moments before His trial and crucifixion. He went to a garden to pray, and "being in an agony he prayed more earnestly; and his sweat became like great drops of blood falling down to the ground" (verse 44). It would be difficult to find a fuller expression of deep sorrow than this. Again, we know Jesus was speaking directly to His Father, and yet He was not alone. The disciples were just a "stone's throw" away (verse 41). Jesus invited His friends into the battle He was facing. He didn't hide the fact that the night was dark and the future looked difficult.

I'm not suggesting we sling the deep sorrow of our hearts out to everyone. It is wise and right to carefully choose those people with whom we share our deepest pain and frustrations. However, I am learning to live more transparently and openly than I have ever lived before, and I'm finding great freedom in it. I'm discovering that people are okay with the real broken-Barbie Bo. My honesty gives them permission to be truthful as well.

In addition, I want my words to build up rather than tear down.

Building Words

When we are in battle, it is not easy to choose life-giving words. We want to unleash our fear and frustration on a tangible villain. At least I do. On some of the most intense or sorrowful days, I have wanted someone to blame in the worst way. Possible punching bags are everywhere: Doctors who don't return phone calls, insurance companies who don't cover the bills from the doctors who don't return phone calls, and well-meaning people who say the wrong thing at the wrong time. And these innocent bystanders are not the only easy targets.

Sometimes I've released my frustration on the people most

precious to me; the very ones I'm fighting for, I find myself fighting against. Nothing makes me sadder than these moments of self-indulgence when I use my pain to justify an outburst or to use cutting words and in the process hurt someone else.

One stressful Thanksgiving, as I worked to get dinner made for a large crowd, my son, who loves to spend time with me in the kitchen, came in to see how he could help. At the same moment, I remembered that Steve has always helped me get the turkey out of the oven, and that he could no longer do so. It's not impossible for me to pull a turkey from the oven, but the realization that this disease has changed life as I have always known it hit me really hard. Instead of taking a minute to breathe deeply and let the sorrow pass, I yelled at Josiah over something silly and small. As soon as I saw the fallen face of my eleven-year-old boy, I was filled with regret so deep and so humiliating that I had to leave the kitchen to cry in my room. Not only did Josiah get an apology that day, but I'm sure he got way more presents at Christmas, too. That day has never left me. It serves as a reminder that words of death cut both ways.

Some of the most unhappy people I know are those who pick the wrong bad guy and use their words to break instead of build. They immerse themselves in sorrow, and bitterness becomes their only comfort. They lash out about every injustice to everyone who will listen, shaking their fist at every perceived villain and spending vital energy in the process. As they wage this war against ex-spouses, bad business partners, or corrupt family members, they sink into the heart of a battle that can never be won and create a lot of collateral damage in the process. It is a sad, draining, and discouraging way to live.

On the flip side, I have a friend at church who is always, always speaking strength into the people around her. She was homeless and addicted to every sort of substance for most of her adult life, and then she found Jesus during her fight with cancer (which she won!). Though her life still would not fit neatly into the category of "easy" or even "comfortable," she is one of the most joy-filled people I know.

I felt beaten up by fear and insecure in my identity when I showed up at a Bible study one day recently. I had cried out that morning for any sort of encouragement. When I walked into the room, a friend came over to greet me with, "Hello, beautiful woman of God!" I almost laughed out loud. She couldn't have picked a less accurate name for me that morning, and her words just bounced off my bad mood without sinking in. But when I hugged her, she added, "He is so wonderful, isn't He, Bo?" Okay, well . . . that's a thought I can agree with. Even at my worst, God is still at His best. "Yes," I said, "He is wonderful," and as soon as my ears heard it, I could feel my heart believing it. Her words came out so easily, like a little river into my dry day, and they were strength for me. Life. Hope. He *is* so wonderful, isn't He?

I want to be like my friend, and so I'm working on the words I say to others, and I'm working on the words I say to myself. While I am committed to being honest about the journey we are on, I also want to use words that connect our hurt to His healing.

One night I found myself spinning a lot of questions and fears about the future through my mind. Rather than push them all to the background and pretend they didn't exist, I got out my computer and listed them, one by one. When I saw them on the page, I realized these big fears were creating a deep well of worry in my life. Reading them, I felt weak and powerless, so I went back and added to each of those fears something that I knew to be true about the love of God. I can't say that I found easy answers for each question, but I did reconnect to all the strength I needed to face the questions with faith. My list included things like this:

Sometimes I worry . . .

. . . that my friends will feel like they're out of encouraging things to say and they'll find new friends on happier journeys. Then I remember who my friends are and what they're made of. End of worry.

. . . that I will miss an important moment, and it will slip through my fingers like water in sand. Then I remember that God is writing everything in His book and I can trust His memory even when I can't trust my own.

. . . that our family, marked by joy for so long, will now be defined by disease or sorrow or loss. Then I look at them. From little to big, I watch them in worship and in conversation, riding bikes, building Legos, working hard, and just living life well, and I know: more than Stern, our name is Loved. I see it in my children most of all. God's work is *always* and *only* beautiful, and it will define us.

. . . that life will never look normal again. Then I remember that He didn't come to make me normal; He came to make me His.

This little list was the first of many like it, some written, some whispered or cried or shouted out in the place of prayer. I do not hesitate to tell God I am hurting, but I am working hard to always add a declaration of His faithfulness. Life is hard, but He is good. His work is always and only beautiful. I love how true words and building words work together to construct something that will stand when everything else shakes.

Proverbs 14:1 says that the wise woman builds her house; the foolish woman tears it down with her own hands. I think that more often than not, we tear our houses down with our own words. We let fear, anxiety, or anger seep into the substructure and eat away at our ability to encourage and build. It's never too late to remodel. It's not too late to speak strength into your heart, your home, and your battlefield.

I am also making it a goal to speak words of worship, words that speak of God's truth and mercy, because these, too, are powerful words of life.

Worship Words

Perhaps the most convenient target for our anger in times of trouble is God Himself. It's easy to lash out at Him with sweeping statements and accusatory questions. It's tempting to question His judgment, His kindness, or His love. Please believe it when I say that this is a dead end. I distinctly remember the twenty-four-hour period when my feet traveled this particular stretch of barren road, and I have never felt more alone or hopeless in my life. It scared me enough to determine that no matter what happened, I would never revisit the idea of God-as-enemy, and I never have.

I don't have all the answers and I will never unravel all the mystery this side of heaven, but here's what I know for sure:

God does not give disease.

He does not destroy marriages or cause affairs or bankruptcy or brokenness.

He is the God of abundant life, but we live in a world that is in a constant state of death and decay. We are huddled together in the gray and grieving here and now, where bodies and hearts break. In His goodness, mercy, and unfailing love, He tends to our wounds and loves us back to life, and then He builds for us a perfect and eternal life beyond the borders of this temporary one.

When I remember who He is and what He's done in my life, all I can do is worship. When I forget, it's hard to speak any positive words. The more I speak of His goodness, His kindness, and His love, the more strength I feel seeping into my bones and marrow and soul. Again, we can trace these worship words back to King David: "Say to God, 'How awesome are your deeds! So great is your power that your enemies come cringing to you'" (Psalm 66:3).

Read that one more time. I love the line, "Say to God." Why does the psalmist want us to tell God these things? Does God need to be reminded about how strong He is or how afraid His enemies are of His muscles? No, I don't think so. I think we are to say it to God because *we* need to be reminded of how strong God is. Here's another one: "Praise our God, you peoples; let the sound of His praise be heard" (Psalm 66:8, HCSB).

Speaking (or singing) the truth of God's strength and power is a beautiful battle strategy. As worship words move from our mouths to our ears and into our hearts, they begin to soften our fear and frustration. They remind us that we are small, but He is big; we are finite, but He is infinite. Worship repositions Him as our God and defender. We can relax our arms, let down our guard, and trust Him to fight for us.

As I walk the soil of this battleground, those around me will get an honest answer to the question *How are you?* I will be transparent when the road is rough, but I am also determined to make sure that my words are building words and that they include a steady stream of honor for God's goodness to me, to my family, and to our world.

This battle strategy is blessing our children and creating a new sense of peace and joy inside a home that might otherwise be suffocating beneath the weight of sorrow. It is the difference between life and death, and I'm so grateful for twenty thousand opportunities to speak strength into the battle that I face every day. I hope to use them well.

WORTH PONDERING

1. What is the most challenging situation in your life? Describe how you generally speak of it.
2. Proverbs 14:1 says, "A wise woman builds her home, but a foolish woman tears it down with her own hands" (NLT). In what ways have you seen women use words to tear down their homes?

WORTH DOING

Pay attention this week to the silent conversations that go on in your head. Are they primarily positive or negative? Strong or weak? Happy or sad? Memorize one verse that you can say out loud to interrupt and upend a negative flow of words in your life. For ideas, see the list of Scriptures for battle in the appendix.

CHAPTER 15

Become Outrageously Brave

Strategic Courage

At the very end of Steve's diagnostic process, when the doctors had eliminated all other possible reasons for his atrophy, they suggested a last resort: a spinal tap. Though I didn't want him to have to endure that painful procedure, I also knew it was our last hope for a different diagnosis. The morning of the spinal tap, I woke up shaking and sick to my stomach. I was as afraid as I have ever been. As I prayed in the darkness of our room, I remembered the following story.

In 1965, my parents were young, in love, and flat broke. While my dad attended Bible college and tried to find work, my mom stayed home with their two little girls, trying hard to make a happy home on a shoestring budget. My parents knew they were doing what God had asked them to do, but it was challenging to trust God for direction and provision. My mom remembers the day that everything ran out. She was trying to make lunch for her little family with a loaf of bread that someone had given them, but she had nothing else. *God,* she pleaded in her tiny kitchen, *how can I give my little girls bread and no butter? You provided the bread. Please could You give us some butter?*

Before she reached *Amen,* in walked my dad, carrying a box of groceries. A widow from their church had been woken up multiple times in the night, hearing the Holy Spirit instruct her to pack up some groceries and give them to my parents. Heart beating fast, my mom began to pull items out of the box, wondering if her prayer had been answered. Finally she saw it. At the bottom of that box sat one half of a cube of butter. It was the most perfect butter she had ever seen. It was more than butter; it was a note from God Himself that said, *I heard you, and I am big enough for your battle.*

Later my mom sought out the woman to thank her for the gift. The kind woman smiled uncomfortably and said, "Oh, Ellen, I'm so embarrassed about that box. You see, I knew that God had said to give you the groceries, so I put several things in from my fridge, but I left the butter on the shelf because, well, it was only half a cube. Before I could bring you the box, I distinctly heard the Lord say, 'Give them the butter, too.' I told Him that I would be glad to go buy you a full pound of butter later in the week but I would be ashamed to put such a small leftover in the box. But He kept insisting that you needed it, so I put it at the very bottom."

When someone in our family is up against a big need or a fierce fight, it is certain that one of us will say, "Remember the half cube of butter? That's the God we serve." For all of my life, mentioning the "half cube of butter" means that we can go ahead and be brave. So I replayed that story in my head as I drove Steve to the hospital. I wrote about it in my journal as I sat in the waiting room. Though my mind wanted to race ahead to the possibilities of all we might be facing, that one little battle story calmed my fear and fueled my faith to know that we would never have to fight alone. That silly cube of butter made me brave. I'm sure my parents would have chosen to avoid that early battlefield of poverty, but that is the ground where God proved His power to them and to those who would follow after them.

Fear is powerful and I want to avoid it. And yet, fearful situations are the ground on which courage is born. The battle pushes us into unknown territory and gives us the opportunity to be wholly dependent on an unchanging God. The God who has always been able is currently able and will always be able to defend us from our darkest enemy. We don't need to convince God to save us or to please, oh, please be strong enough to intervene. We need to convince *ourselves* that He is able, and that fight starts in our minds.

NO WAY OUT

Let's return for a moment to the story of David and Goliath in 1 Samuel 17. The scene is this: The Israelites had been camping out in the Valley of Elah. They were lined up in battle formation, ready to face the Philistines, when Goliath lifted up all nine feet, nine inches of his hulking frame and bellowed this challenge to the Israelites: "'I defy the ranks of Israel today. Send me a man so we can fight each other!' When Saul and all Israel heard these words from the Philistine, they lost their courage and were terrified" (verses 10-11, HCSB).

These soldiers were prepared and waiting to fight the Philistine army, but when the battle was suddenly reduced to one big bully, they all started shaking in their boots. Goliath effectively narrowed the conflict down to a fight-to-the-death, man-to-man battle. The Israelites were no longer asking, "Will *we* win?" but rather, "Will *I* die? How much will it hurt? How long will it take?"

When we get separated from the rest of our army, we're easier to scare. Goliath got these soldiers to project ahead and imagine what might happen out on the battlefield against a bully of his size and strength, and what they envisioned was terrifying. The Israelite soldiers had many reasons to be afraid of a showdown with this supersized enemy, but they were faced with another big problem as well: There was no other way out.

Ever been there? I can't tell you how many times I've awakened in the morning feeling happy and peaceful, and then I suddenly remember the fight that our family is in. If I fail to invite the voice of the Holy Spirit into that moment, I will inevitably begin to hear Goliath taunting me from the sidelines, reminding me that we have no exit strategy. That's when my mind races to all that we could encounter up ahead, and I panic. I am stuck in the Valley of Elah with just two options: fall on my sword, or face this fight with faith in the God who is strong enough to take on this giant. Saul and his men were in this same situation. They had heard the threats of the enemy, they had imagined what would happen if they faced Goliath on the battle-field, and they were immobilized by fear.

Day after day for *forty* days the army lined up in formation until Goliath shouted them down. Same trick, and it worked every time. In fact, verse 24 says that the giant's blustery words sent the men running, terrified. That must have been a good time for Goliath, but I'm sure not one Israelite woke up in the morning thinking, *Today I really want to look stupid, so I'm going to go out, face that giant, and then run like a girl when he yells at us.* None of us *wants* to be cowardly, but our desire for self-preservation is powerful, and it pushes us to do things we wouldn't do if our thoughts were aligned with the purposes of God. As long as we're focused on what our enemy could do to us, we're vulnerable to making bad decisions.

THE SECRET TO DAVID'S COURAGE

The day that David visited his brothers in the camp, everything changed. He brought them not only food but also a fresh, new perspective on what was really going on. Verse 22 tells us that David "ran to the battle line" (HCSB). Quite a contrast, when the rest of the army had forty times run *away* from it. David faced the same giant and had access to the same facts about Goliath's strength and prowess, and yet when he rolled the picture in his mind ten minutes forward, he saw it playing out differently than the rest of the soldiers did. They imagined themselves dying a painful death, but he saw himself carrying the bloody head of his enemy. David faced the same battle as everyone else, but his picture of the future was remarkably optimistic. Why? When all of these trained warriors were shaking in their boots, what caused David to respond in a way that was outrageously brave? I believe it's because before he moved his thoughts forward, he moved them backward. Look at his response to Saul when he was told that fighting Goliath would be a suicide mission:

> Your servant used to keep sheep for his father [backward]. And when there came a lion, or a bear, and took a lamb from the flock, I went after him and struck him and delivered it out of his mouth [backward]. And if he arose against me, I caught him by his beard and struck him and killed him [backward]. Your servant has struck down both lions and bears [backward], and this uncircumcised Philistine shall be like one of them [forward!], for he has defied the armies of the living God. (verses 34-36)

This may seem as though David were relying heavily on his own abilities, but keep reading . . .

> The Lord who delivered me from the paw of the lion and from the paw of the bear will deliver me from the hand of this Philistine [forward!]. (verse 37)

What was David doing? He was going backward in order to go forward with courage. He was remembering how in the past God had given him supernatural power to defend the helpless, and that bolstered his faith that God would do it again this time. In essence he said that if God gave him the strength to protect a simple sheep, surely He would empower David to defeat a giant who defied His own name. David reminded himself of the character of God, which enabled him to align his view of the future with God's view, and that resulted in some outrageous bravery. Brilliant.

FILLING YOUR MEMORY BANKS

I know of no better way to gain courage to face whatever battle is up ahead of you than to replay all the things that God has already done for you. Rehearse them. Recount them. Talk about them. Write them down. Let them sink so solidly into your mind-set that no bully of any size could ever separate you from them.

And make these courage-soaked Scriptures your own:

> If you say in your heart, "These nations are greater than I. How can I dispossess them?" you shall not be afraid of them but *you shall remember* what the Lord your God did to Pharaoh and to all Egypt, the great trials that your eyes saw, the signs, the wonders, the mighty hand, and the outstretched arm, by which the Lord your God brought

you out. So will the LORD your God do to all the peoples of whom you are afraid. (Deuteronomy 7:17-19, emphasis added)

You shall not forget the covenant that I have made with you. You shall not fear other gods, but you shall fear the LORD your God, and he will deliver you out of the hand of all your enemies. (2 Kings 17:38-39, emphasis added)

I am deeply depressed; *therefore I remember* You from the land of Jordan and the peaks of Hermon, from Mount Mizar. (Psalm 42:6, HCSB, emphasis added)

My soul, praise the LORD, and *do not forget* all His benefits. (Psalm 103:2, HCSB, emphasis added)

I will never forget Your precepts, for You have given me life through them. . . . The wicked hope to destroy me, but *I contemplate* Your decrees. (Psalm 119:93,95, HCSB, emphasis added)

These verses only scratch the surface of this subject. Psalm 136 is devoted to the recitation of the great works of God so that the next generations of the children of Israel, who didn't experience these acts of deliverance firsthand, would have courage to trust Him no matter what enemy they encountered. If you want to face your current battle with faith rather than fear, go back and remember the good things God has done in our world and in your life.

I have begun to build a list I am calling One Hundred Reasons to Be Brave. It chronicles the amazing things God has done for me and my family and the ways He has strengthened and helped us time and time again. This is not just a list of things I'm thankful for; it's a résumé of the miraculous things that only God could have been responsible for in our lives.

Item number one: As Steve, Whitney, and I traveled over a winding mountain pass in 1988, our car was hit head-on by a drunk driver. By all accounts, our daughter, who was just thirteen months old at the time, should have been killed in that accident, but she escaped with some facial scarring and we all gained a fresh gratitude for traveling mercies. God did that.

Item number two: Steve was between jobs. We had two children, no money, and no groceries left in the house. Though we were not ashamed to ask our families for help, Steve and I felt that we were supposed to wait to see what God would do. The doorbell rang, but when we opened it, no one was there. On our doorstep were six bags of groceries . . . and Oreo cookies. Only God.

And one more: One morning early in our battle, I woke up feeling anxious. We hadn't yet told anyone outside of our families what we were facing, and I felt myself sinking in the mud of fear and worry. For the first time in as long as I could remember, I wondered where God was. I couldn't find Him or feel Him. I couldn't hear Him or see Him. I was bereft and felt as if I was losing not just Steve but also my grip on grace.

I cried in my car on the way to work and I prayed, *Please, Jesus, I just need to know that there is grace for this. I just need to know.* I hid myself in my office, where I could ride out the storm and not have to explain anything to anyone. As I tried unsuccessfully to focus on the words on my computer screen, I heard a tap on my door. I looked up to see a friend who had come to the church to meet with someone else. He comes to the church often, as he is a man of wisdom and helps us make good decisions, but he rarely stops by my office without a reason. I motioned for him to come in; he cracked the door a bit, looked at me for a long moment, and then said quietly, but with great depth of meaning, "Grace to you, Bo Stern." I was longing for grace, and God sent grace. He packaged it up in the heart and words of a man I trust, and He sent it straight to my office. God broke into my sadness and sorrow, interrupted my hiding, and sent grace into that moment. It's a miracle if ever I have experienced one. It's a miracle as magnificent as six bags of groceries or ten thousand dollars.

When God shows up, you just know it. You feel it. And when He shows up, things change. When God's power intersects with our need, we must not only use it for the crisis at hand but also put it into a memory bank so we can face the fearsome fights that are ahead. These powerful interventions can give us courage and confidence to face the next battle with great faith.

WORTH PONDERING

1. Who is the bravest person you know?
2. Revelation 12:11 tells us that one way we can overcome our enemy is by the "word of [our] testimony." Why do you suppose our testimonies are such a powerful weapon in war?

WORTH DOING

Take a few minutes and start your own One Hundred Reasons to Be Brave list. Remember God's goodness in your life. Recount His blessings. Build a résumé for His character by refusing to forget what He has done. Having trouble getting started? Start with the fact that God chose you to be born on this earth and to reach to you and call you His own. Is there a time when you should have died? You are still here, living and breathing. This is a reason for courage. Was there a moment when you felt like giving up but just the right encouragement came at exactly the right time? Another reason for some brilliant bravery.

Conclusion

As we near the end of our journey together, I feel the mixed emotions that come at the end of a family reunion. We are fellow soldiers, facing futures that are filled with fearsome giants and powerful possibilities. I'm so glad we've spent this time together. Many things are uncertain on our battlefields, but this much we know: We march in step behind a brilliant Commander. He is not just a good God or a loving God; He is a *winning* God. When He fights, He wins, and if He is in our fight, then we will win too.

Steve and I are still in the middle of this battle, and I do not know how or when it will end. Consequently, I have no neatly wrapped-up resolutions, only in-the-trenches truth. As I've considered what is most important in the fight up ahead, two points shine like beacons on a dense, dark night. Everything in all of life boils down to knowing these two truths in this exact order:

1. God is for you, with you, and crazy about you.
2. If you let Him, He will use this battle to make you more beautiful than you ever dreamed you could be.

That's it. That's the beginning and end, and if you have those two things woven into the fabric of your spirit, then you, my friend, have everything. Even if your fight leads to physical death, you can know that it will ultimately lead to abundant and eternal life. The words of Paul ring as true today as they did for the early church. They are as fitting when facing the giant of ALS as they were for those facing Nero.

> In all these things we are more than conquerors through him who loved us. For I am sure that neither death nor life, nor angels nor rulers, nor things present nor things to come, nor powers, nor height nor depth, nor anything else in all creation, will be able to separate us from the love of God in Christ Jesus our Lord. (Romans 8:37-39)

Fight on, beautiful soldier. The Lord goes before you, and He is strong enough for every giant.

Scriptures for Battle

WHEN YOU FEEL OVERMATCHED IN BATTLE:

Deuteronomy 20:1 — When you go out to war against your enemies, and see horses and chariots and an army larger than your own, you shall not be afraid of them, for the LORD your God is with you, who brought you up out of the land of Egypt.

2 Chronicles 32:7-8 — "Be strong and courageous. Do not be afraid or dismayed before the king of Assyria and all the horde that is with him, for there are more with us than with him. With him is an arm of flesh, but with us is the LORD our God, to help us and to fight our battles." And the people took confidence from the words of Hezekiah king of Judah.

Psalm 18:16-19 — He sent from on high, he took me; he drew me out of many waters. He rescued me from my strong enemy and from those who hated me, for they were too mighty for me. They confronted me in the day of my calamity, but the LORD was my support. He brought me out into a broad place; he rescued me, because he delighted in me.

Psalm 91:3-6 — He will deliver you from the snare of the fowler and from the deadly pestilence. He will cover you with his pinions, and under his wings you will find refuge; his faithfulness is a shield and buckler. You will not fear the terror of the night, nor the arrow that flies by day, nor the pestilence that stalks in darkness, nor the destruction that wastes at noonday.

Matthew 11:28-30 — Come to me, all who labor and are heavy laden, and I will give you rest. Take my yoke upon you, and learn from me, for I am gentle and lowly in heart, and you will find rest for your souls. For my yoke is easy, and my burden is light.

1 Corinthians 15:57 — Thanks be to God, who gives us the victory through our Lord Jesus Christ.

2 Corinthians 4:7-10 — We have this treasure in jars of clay, to show that the surpassing power belongs to God and not to us. We are afflicted in every way, but not crushed; perplexed, but not driven to despair; persecuted, but not forsaken; struck down, but not destroyed; always carrying in the body the death of Jesus, so that the life of Jesus may also be manifested in our bodies.

WHEN YOU FEEL ALONE IN BATTLE:

Deuteronomy 31:8 — It is the LORD who goes before you. He will be with you; he will not leave you or forsake you. Do not fear or be dismayed.

Psalm 18:6 — In my distress I called upon the LORD; to my God I cried for help. From his temple he heard my voice, and my cry to him reached his ears.

Psalm 139:7-12 — Where shall I go from your Spirit? Or where shall I flee from your presence? If I ascend to heaven, you are there! If I make my bed in Sheol, you are there! If I take the wings of the morning and dwell in the uttermost parts of the sea, even there your hand shall lead me, and your right hand shall hold me. If I say,

"Surely the darkness shall cover me, and the light about me be night," even the darkness is not dark to you; the night is bright as the day, for darkness is as light with you.

Proverbs 18:24—A man of many companions may come to ruin, but there is a friend who sticks closer than a brother.

Hosea 2:14-15—Behold, I will allure her, and bring her into the wilderness, and speak tenderly to her. And there I will give her her vineyards and make the Valley of Achor a door of hope. And there she shall answer as in the days of her youth, as at the time when she came out of the land of Egypt.

Matthew 28:20—Behold, I am with you always, to the end of the age.

Romans 8:38-39—I am sure that neither death nor life, nor angels nor rulers, nor things present nor things to come, nor powers, nor height nor depth, nor anything else in all creation, will be able to separate us from the love of God in Christ Jesus our Lord.

WHEN YOU NEED PEACE IN BATTLE:

Psalm 4:8—In peace I will both lie down and sleep; for you alone, O LORD, make me dwell in safety.

Psalm 46:1-3—God is our refuge and strength, a very present help in trouble. Therefore we will not fear though the earth gives way, though the mountains be moved into the heart of the sea, though its waters roar and foam, though the mountains tremble at its swelling.

Psalm 46:9-10—He makes wars cease to the end of the earth; he breaks the bow and shatters the spear; he burns the chariots with fire. "Be still, and know that I am God. I will be exalted among the nations, I will be exalted in the earth!"

Psalm 56:3-4 — When I am afraid, I put my trust in you. In God, whose word I praise, in God I trust; I shall not be afraid. What can flesh do to me?

Psalm 119:76 — Let your steadfast love comfort me according to your promise to your servant.

Proverbs 3:23-24 — You will walk on your way securely, and your foot will not stumble. If you lie down, you will not be afraid; when you lie down, your sleep will be sweet.

Isaiah 55:10-12 — As the rain and the snow come down from heaven and do not return there but water the earth, making it bring forth and sprout, giving seed to the sower and bread to the eater, so shall my word be that goes out from my mouth; it shall not return to me empty, but it shall accomplish that which I purpose, and shall succeed in the thing for which I sent it. For you shall go out in joy and be led forth in peace; the mountains and the hills before you shall break forth into singing, and all the trees of the field shall clap their hands.

John 14:27 — Peace I leave with you; my peace I give to you. Not as the world gives do I give to you. Let not your hearts be troubled, neither let them be afraid.

Philippians 4:6-7 — Do not be anxious about anything, but in everything by prayer and supplication with thanksgiving let your requests be made known to God. And the peace of God, which surpasses all understanding, will guard your hearts and your minds in Christ Jesus.

WHEN YOU NEED STRENGTH IN BATTLE:

Exodus 15:2 — The LORD is my strength and my song, and he has become my salvation.

Judges 5:21 — March on, my soul, with might!

2 Samuel 22:40 — You equipped me with strength for the battle; you made those who rise against me sink under me.

Psalm 28:7-8 — The LORD is my strength and my shield; in him my heart trusts, and I am helped; my heart exults, and with my song I give thanks to him. The LORD is the strength of his people; he is the saving refuge of his anointed.

Psalm 84:5-7 — Blessed are those whose strength is in you, in whose heart are the highways to Zion. As they go through the Valley of Baca they make it a place of springs; the early rain also covers it with pools. They go from strength to strength; each one appears before God in Zion.

Habakkuk 3:19 — GOD, the Lord, is my strength; he makes my feet like the deer's; he makes me tread on my high places.

WHEN YOU NEED ENDURANCE IN BATTLE:

Romans 15:4-6 — Whatever was written in former days was written for our instruction, that through endurance and through the encouragement of the Scriptures we might have hope. May the God of endurance and encouragement grant you to live in such harmony with one another, in accord with Christ Jesus, that together you may with one voice glorify the God and Father of our Lord Jesus Christ.

2 Corinthians 6:4-10—As servants of God we commend ourselves in every way: by great endurance, in afflictions, hardships, calamities, beatings, imprisonments, riots, labors, sleepless nights, hunger; by purity, knowledge, patience, kindness, the Holy Spirit, genuine love; by truthful speech, and the power of God; with the weapons of righteousness for the right hand and for the left; through honor and dishonor, through slander and praise. We are treated as impostors, and yet are true; as unknown, and yet well known; as dying, and behold, we live; as punished, and yet not killed; as sorrowful, yet always rejoicing; as poor, yet making many rich; as having nothing, yet possessing everything.

Colossians 1:11-12—May you be strengthened with all power, according to his glorious might, for all endurance and patience with joy, giving thanks to the Father, who has qualified you to share in the inheritance of the saints in light.

James 1:2-4—Dear brothers and sisters, when troubles come your way, consider it an opportunity for great joy. For you know that when your faith is tested, your endurance has a chance to grow. So let it grow, for when your endurance is fully developed, you will be perfect and complete, needing nothing. (NLT)

WHEN YOU NEED CONFIDENCE IN BATTLE:

Psalm 71:5—You have been my hope, O Sovereign LORD, my confidence since my youth. (NIV)

Proverbs 3:25-26—Do not be afraid of sudden terror or of the ruin of the wicked, when it comes, for the LORD will be your confidence and will keep your foot from being caught.

Isaiah 32:17-18 — The effect of righteousness will be peace, and the result of righteousness, quietness and trust forever. My people will abide in a peaceful habitation, in secure dwellings, and in quiet resting places.

Jeremiah 17:7-8 — Blessed is the man who trusts in the LORD, whose trust is the LORD. He is like a tree planted by water, that sends out its roots by the stream, and does not fear when heat comes, for its leaves remain green, and is not anxious in the year of drought, for it does not cease to bear fruit.

Ephesians 3:11-12 — This was according to the eternal purpose that he has realized in Christ Jesus our Lord, in whom we have boldness and access with confidence through our faith in him.

Hebrews 10:35-36 — Therefore do not throw away your confidence, which has a great reward. For you have need of endurance, so that when you have done the will of God you may receive what is promised.

WHEN YOU NEED JOY IN BATTLE:

Psalm 5:11 — But let all who take refuge in you rejoice; let them ever sing for joy, and spread your protection over them, that those who love your name may exult in you.

Psalm 16:9-11 — Therefore my heart is glad, and my whole being rejoices; my flesh also dwells secure. For you will not abandon my soul to Sheol, or let your holy one see corruption. You make known to me the path of life; in your presence there is fullness of joy; at your right hand are pleasures forevermore.

Psalm 20:5 — May we shout for joy over your salvation, and in the name of our God set up our banners! May the LORD fulfill all your petitions!

Isaiah 12:3,5-6 — With joy you will draw water from the wells of salvation. . . . "Sing praises to the LORD, for he has done gloriously; let this be made known in all the earth. Shout, and sing for joy, O inhabitant of Zion, for great in your midst is the Holy One of Israel."

Isaiah 51:11 — And the ransomed of the LORD shall return and come to Zion with singing; everlasting joy shall be upon their heads; they shall obtain gladness and joy, and sorrow and sighing shall flee away.

Isaiah 61:1-3 — The Spirit of the Lord GOD is upon me . . . to proclaim liberty to the captives, and the opening of the prison to those who are bound; to proclaim the year of the LORD's favor, and the day of vengeance of our God; to comfort all who mourn; to grant to those who mourn in Zion — to give them a beautiful headdress instead of ashes, the oil of gladness instead of mourning, the garment of praise instead of a faint spirit.

Notes

Chapter 3: Catching Manna

1. The ten plagues of Egypt are found in Exodus 7–12, and the parting of the Red Sea is found in Exodus 14.
2. Edward McKendree Bounds, *The Necessity of Prayer* (Grand Rapids, MI: Baker, 1976), 7.

Chapter 5: What the Greeting Cards Won't Tell You

1. See Luke 22:42.

Chapter 6: Wearing the Glasses of God

1. See Exodus 14; 16–17.
2. See Exodus 13:21-22.

Chapter 7: An Unlikely Dance

1. James Strong, *Strong's Exhaustive Concordance of the Bible* (Nashville: Thomas Nelson, 1990), 67.
2. Strong, 83.
3. See 1 John 5:19.

Chapter 9: Consult the Captain

1. This e-mail message is used with permission.

Chapter 10: Get a Good Army
1. E-mail message to author. Used with permission.

Chapter 12: Run to a Reliable Refuge
1. James Strong, *Strong's Exhaustive Concordance of the Bible* (Nashville: Thomas Nelson, 1990), 42.
2. Strong, 140.

Chapter 13: Escape the Weight of Bitterness
1. I changed the name and identifying details to protect the identity of this person.
2. James Strong, *Strong's Exhaustive Concordance of the Bible* (Nashville: Thomas Nelson, 1990), 3.

Chapter 14: Speak Strength
1. Dr. Louann Brizendine, interview with *Good Morning America*, August 7, 2006.

About the Author

BO STERN is a persuasive, sought-after speaker and writer. Her role as a teaching pastor at Westside Church in Bend, Oregon, gives her a platform to share her personal journey and deep insight into the heart of God. Her message of hope compels others to seek God in a more intimate way. She possesses a unique gift of taking complex theology and expressing it through simple, personal illustration.

Bo has been married to her wonderful husband, Steve, for twenty-seven years, and together they have raised four amazing kids. They serve together on the international board of directors for Kings Kids Village, a home for AIDS-affected orphans in Nairobi, Kenya. She is also heavily involved in raising awareness and funding for ALS research.

To find out more about Bo, visit www.bostern.com.

More powerful books on issues for women from NavPress.

Celibate Sex
Abbie Smith

Get a fresh look at sexuality from the perspective of a Christian who is single. Abbie Smith teaches you about sex and sexuality, purity and longing, intimacy and union with God on a non-theologian view of singleness, and how God is calling you to be in union with Him.

978-1-61291-353-7

Every Thought Captive
Jerusha Clark

Every Thought Captive explores the unique nature of the female mind and examines the sources of our fears and anxieties. Drawing from personal experiences, including struggles with anorexia and depression, best-selling author Jerusha Clark shares the freedom found in shifting our thoughts from the everyday to the eternal.

978-1-57683-868-6

The Life You Crave
Jerusha Clark

Everyone desires God's best for her life, but in a world of ever-expanding options and lots of advice, what is the best way to pursue a life well lived? Author Jerusha Clark believes that God has given us the gift of discernment, which will lead us to what is truly His best.

978-1-60006-055-7

To order copies, call NavPress at **1-800-366-7788** or log on to **www.NavPress.com**.

NAVPRESS

Discipleship Inside Out®